Permission to Steal

Revealing the Roots of Corporate Scandal
An Address to My Fellow Citizens

Lisa H. Newton

Blackwell
Publishing

© 2006 by Lisa H. Newton

BLACKWELL PUBLISHING
350 Main Street, Malden, MA 02148-5020, USA
9600 Garsington Road, Oxford OX4 2DQ, UK
550 Swanston Street, Carlton, Victoria 3053, Australia

The right of Lisa H. Newton to be identified as the Author of this Work has been asserted
in accordance with the UK Copyright, Designs, and Patents Act 1988.

First published 2006 by Blackwell Publishing Ltd

1   2006

Library of Congress Cataloging-in-Publication Data

Newton, Lisa H., 1939–
    Permission to steal : revealing the roots of corporate scandal / Lisa H. Newton.
        p. cm. — (Blackwell public philosophy)
    Includes bibliographical references and index.
    ISBN-13: 978-1-4051-4539-8 (hardback : alk. paper)
    ISBN-10: 1-4051-4539-0 (hardback : alk. paper)
    ISBN-13: 978-1-4051-4540-4 (pbk. : alk. paper)
    ISBN-10: 1-4051-4540-4 (pbk. : alk. paper) 1. White collar crimes—United States.
2. Corporations—Corrupt practices—United States. 3. Corporations—Moral and ethical
aspects. 4. Corporate culture—Moral and ethical aspects. 5. Business ethics—United States.
I. Title. II. Series.

    HV6769.N49 2006
    364.16′80973—dc22

                                                                        2006016595

A catalogue record for this title is available from the British Library.

Set in 11/13.5 Dante
by Graphicraft Limited, Hong Kong
Printed and bound in Singapore
by COS Printers Pte Ltd

The publisher's policy is to use permanent paper from mills that operate a sustainable
forestry policy, and which has been manufactured from pulp processed using acid-free and
elementary chlorine-free practices. Furthermore, the publisher ensures that the text paper
and cover board used have met acceptable environmental accreditation standards.

For further information on
Blackwell Publishing, visit our website:
www.blackwellpublishing.com

Lisa H. Newton is Professor of Philosophy and Director of the Program in Applied Ethics at Fairfield University. She is the author of numerous articles and books in business ethics, and most recently published *Business Ethics and the Natural Environment* (Blackwell, 2004).

Blackwell Public Philosophy

Edited by Michael Boylan, Marymount University

In a world of 24-hour news cycles and increasingly specialized knowledge, the Blackwell Public Philosophy series takes seriously the idea that there is a need and demand for engaging and thoughtful discussion of topics of broad public importance. Philosophy itself is historically grounded in the public square, bringing people together to try to understand the various issues that shape their lives and give them meaning. This "love of wisdom" – the essence of philosophy – lies at the heart of the series. Written in an accessible, jargon-free manner by internationally renowned authors, each book is an invitation to the world beyond news flashes and sound bites and into public wisdom.

Permission to Steal: Revealing the Roots of Corporate Scandal by Lisa H. Newton

Forthcoming:

Terrorism and Counter-Terrorism by Seumas Miller
The Extinction of Desire: A Novel Approach to Buddhism by Michael Boylan
Evil On-Line: Explorations of Evil and Wickedness on the Web by Dean Cocking and Jeroen van den Hoven

Contents

CONTENTS

Preface

For those who treasure justice, this time has its peculiar satisfactions. As I write this preface, some time after completing the text of this book, Kenneth Lay and Jeffrey Skilling have just been convicted of fraud and conspiracy. When last heard from, imprisoned Dennis Kozlowski was attempting to get his insurance company to cover his $17.8 million in legal costs, even as he agreed to pay the state of New York $21.2 million in evaded taxes. WorldCom CEO Bernard Ebbers was sentenced to 25 years in prison, John and Timothy Rigas were also sentenced to jail. Enron CFO Andy Fastow not only is serving time in jail, but I understand that he may not be able to hold on to his enormous mansion in Texas, built specifically to sink his ill-gotten gains into something that could not be taken away. His wife has already served her sentence for her part in the Enron fraud.

The sentencing of Lay and Skilling, undoubted poster children for the evil committed by the overprivileged at the expense of the overtrusting, is scheduled for September 11, 2006. The date is symbolically correct. It is five years to the day since our world changed forever, in the collapse, in terrorist attack, of the towering symbols of our financial supremacy, and the nation will never trust the air again. Lay and Skilling and all the others flew their greed into the centuries-old fabric of the business system, and watched our trust in the entire enterprise fall in pieces. We are diminished, our world is less safe, and we are understandably unhappy; no one likes to be told that the oaks against which we have leaned are but broken reeds. We have been betrayed, and our lives are the poorer for the terrible loss of trust.

But in the end, in another sense, we are the better for it. We assumed that all that we had built was sound and strong and safe, and that we could attend to our work, games, and shopping without thinking about them. Now we know what we long have recited, that eternal vigilance is the price of liberty, not to mention the price of the integrity of our business system. We have watched the disgrace, conviction, and imprisonment of people who were not necessarily bad, they just needed watching – they needed *us* to be watching, and we were not. We must not make that mistake again.

Why do we have to watch, and how shall we do it? This short book attempts to answer those questions.

Introduction: The Stories

Reality is a collection of stories. Theory contemplates those stories, turns them this way and that, looking for trails of truth that lead through all of them, trails that connect them in some way that makes sense. The stories that we contemplate in this brief reflection are about fabulously wealthy businessmen who held responsible positions as executives (for the most part chief executives) in leading companies in the United States in the last decade of the twentieth century, extending into the twenty-first. A second Gay Nineties, a second Gilded Age, came abruptly to an end with their exposure as criminals (or close to it), their fall from power, and their richly deserved subsequent disgrace. As I write this short book, the scandals are by no means over (much of the ill-gotten wealth is still in the hands of those who made off with it), and the high-flying executives are only beginning to come to justice. Appeals will follow. But we know enough to get started on the contemplating, and given that the ill-gotten money was (eventually) ours, we ought to be interested in finding out why we lost it. Just maybe, we can find ways to protect ourselves from the thieves in the next generation, and possibly find a way to educate our children that will make them less likely to become those thieves. Those are two different tasks, note.

First we have to know the stories. I cannot tell any of them in any detail, but then, I don't have to; each of them has been given loving attention by the enthusiastic corps of business journalists, and an appended reading list for the aficionado (see the Bibliography) will provide hours of fun for anyone interested in pursuing them. But we have to have some idea of the central tale and cast of characters for at least the major stories, so that we may refer to them in what follows.

Enron, first and most famous, started as a humble pipeline company; it owned pipes and it transported natural gas. Kenneth Lay became CEO of Houston Natural Gas, one of the predecessor companies, and rapidly parlayed several good friendships in the Republican administration of Ronald Reagan into a relaxation of the regulations that had kept the energy industry from profitable innovations. He named the company Enron in 1985, at the merger of HNG and Internorth. Starting with energy contracts – electricity, gas, and the infrastructure to support them – Enron rapidly expanded into foreign gambles in India and Africa, highly profitable risk management derivatives, including weather derivatives, and discovered new and original ways to conceal company losses (when the gambles failed) by creating "special purpose entities" (SPEs), offshore partnerships, most of which were not quite legal. When the whole structure fell apart, investors lost about $70 billion. (The notorious "Nigerian Barges" scam alone cost them $13.7 million.) The CFO, Andrew Fastow, went to jail, as did his wife (she was released in June 2005); at this writing Kenneth Lay has been indicted but not yet tried. Enron investors promptly sued to get their money back; they did not sue Enron, which had no money, but all the banks that had lent Enron money, on the theory that if the banks had been paying attention, the whole debacle would not have happened. (The lawsuits clearly work; on June 14, 2005, J. P. Morgan Chase agreed to pay the investors $2.2 billion in compensation, following an agreement by Citigroup to pay them $2 billion.[1] On August 2 of that year, Canadian Imperial Bank of Commerce agreed to pay $2.4 billion, setting some kind of record, to settle claims that it helped hide losses at the Enron Corporation, raising to $7.1 billion the settlements to compensate investors.[2] It's a start.)

Enron exemplifies one of the major lingering problems in the entire corporate scandal. When Enron stock was at its peak, shortly before the final decline and fall, Lou Pai, an Enron executive, sold his shares for $350 million and retired from Enron to move to Hawaii where, as far as I know, he still lives, at peace with himself, his neighbors, and the law. After the final collapse, most Enron employees, some of whom had been with the company or its predecessors for many years, discovered that their comfortable retirements had evaporated in the Houston heat, and that they were left with nothing to show for lifetimes of work. On the model enforced by the courts on Bernard Ebbers (see WorldCom, below) it may be possible to extract some reparations for the employees from the personal wealth of Andrew Fastow and (possibly) Kenneth Lay – always excluding Fastow's enormous mansion, which is protected from bankruptcy proceedings by Texas's

---

[1] Julie Creswell, "J. P. Morgan Chase to Pay Enron Investors $2.2 Billion," *The New York Times*, June 15, 2005, first Business Page.
[2] Jeff Bailey, "CIBC Pays to Settle Enron Case: An Agreement for $2.4 Billion," *The New York Times*, August 3, 2005.

Homestead law. But is there any principle on which we can approach Lou Pai, and ask him to give up, maybe, $200 million of the money he got from his Enron holdings, to divide among the employees that Enron cheated out of their savings? We want to think about that.

Arthur Andersen came down with Enron. As the accounting firm that had signed off on all those marvelous deals, those SPEs with shadowed ownership, Andersen had clearly violated the high standard of integrity set for it by its founder, who had assured the Securities and Exchange Commission that the personal integrity of the accountants would be enough to guarantee the integrity of the auditing enterprise. For 60 years, personal integrity had indeed been enough, and Andersen was known as the most unflinchingly upright in the business. But it failed in the Enron case.

A look at the pressures on Andersen, after it had collapsed, revealed the reason for its failure in the Enron era. Since 1929 (and before) independent accounting firms like Andersen have audited the financial reports of all major companies, making sure that they did the addition right, put entries on the proper line, and above all accounted for every dollar in profit, loss, debt, or investment. The auditor's job, essentially, was to rain on your parade if you were trying little schemes to avoid taxes or conceal losses from investors, and to certify you clean and virtuous if you were not. But times had changed; in addition to the essential, unglamorous, and ill-rewarded work of auditing, the major accounting companies had taken on the lucrative work of consulting (mostly on taxes and accounting regulations) with the companies they were auditing. Andersen had just suffered a devastating split: its consultants had announced that they were no longer interested in sharing their stipends throughout the firm (the custom in accounting companies), so went off on their own, leaving Andersen, alone among the Big Five, dependent on auditing income alone. The auditors tasked their new CEO, Joe Berardino, with building up a new consulting business, and he did that, but relied heavily on one major consulting client, Enron, who was also, of course, a very major accounting client. Now, any auditor nastiness, any attempts to rain on Enron's parade, on the permissibility of those SPE deals, might result in the loss of the consulting client, and there goes the business. So Andersen, dependent upon Enron for its consulting trade, was nice about the deals.

In a fit of nervousness, probably about its previous niceness, Andersen's Houston office, the one that ministered to Enron, decided that its Enron records were best not seen by anyone, so it shredded them, bag after bag, over one weekend, handing out huge plastic bags to its employees to take home for guinea pig litter. Possibly the Andersen employees never intended to destroy evidence for the case that was building against Enron and would surely involve Andersen before it was through. Possibly. But everyone on the scene drew the obvious conclusions, and Andersen ended up convicted of conspiracy. The company went out of business immediately. (The conviction was later reversed, but too late to save the company.[3])

The **WorldCom** scandal is a tale of two companies: **MCI**, which had been part of the deregulatory push that broke up the old AT&T telephone monopoly, and became one of the leading communications companies in the United States, and WorldCom itself, a long-distance communications carrier (essentially, an outgrowth of the same AT&T breakup). At one point WorldCom was the United States's second largest long distance carrier,

[3] Charles Lane, "Justices Overturn Andersen Conviction," *Washington Post*, June 1, 2005, p. A1.

AT&T remaining the largest. At this point it has officially disappeared from the books; it went into bankruptcy in July 2002, after finding about $11 billion in accounting fraud on its books. It abandoned its CEO, Bernard Ebbers, to the clutches of the law, and emerged from bankruptcy in April 2003 as **MCI**, the company that it had purchased for $37 billion in 1997. On March 15, 2005, Ebbers was convicted of conspiracy, securities fraud, and false regulatory filings. On July 13, 2005, he was sentenced to 25 years in prison, the longest sentence so far.[4] The huge wealth of the corporation provides no stability in the titanic battles of wealth; someone is convinced that there is even more money out there to be made, and financial maneuvers can keep a company "in play" indefinitely.

One element of the justice question was settled in the Ebbers case, possibly to become a model for the others: on June 30, 2005, Ebbers agreed to give over ("cough up," in the language of the day) all his assets, now about $40 million, to spread among the victims of his frauds. The list of assets to be put at the court's disposal is enlightening: a multimillion dollar income tax refund, assorted properties in Mississippi: 300,000 acres of timber property, a sawmill and lumber concern, KLLM Transport Services in Richland, Sunset Marina in Jackson, Marriott Courtyard in Tupelo, the Brookhaven Country Club in Brookhaven, and 800 acres in Pine Ridge, including his home. There was also a 28,000 acre farm in Louisiana.[5] At one point Ebbers had been worth almost $1 billion; it's a shame the fraud could not have been discovered then.

[4] Ken Belson, "WorldCom Head Is Given 25 Years For Huge Fraud," *The New York Times*, July 14, 2005, A1, C4.
[5] Gretchen Morgenson, "Ebbers Set to Shed His Assets: $40 Million to Go To Fraud Victims," *The New York Times*, July 1, 2005, C1, C6.

Adelphia Communications was the sixth largest cable company in America at one point, but not all of its wealth was real; in 2002 it too went bankrupt. On June 20, 2005, Adelphia's CEO John Rigas was convicted of looting the company of hundreds of millions of dollars and perpetrating a major fraud on the investors; he was sentenced to 15 years in prison. His son, Timothy Rigas, CFO of the company, was sentenced to 20 years; the father got off more lightly because he is 80 years old and suffering from cancer. (Another son, Michael, will be tried later for an associated securities fraud.) Apparently the Rigases had adopted an accounting system so complicated that no one could understand what they were doing, and behind the screen created by the system, they looted the company of up to $2.3 billion.[6]

Tyco was started in 1960 as a laboratory operating on government contracts. By 1964 the company had gone public and developed an appetite for other companies; by the year 1999 it had 260,000 employees and was a highly diversified manufacturing company. Like many companies, it began in that year to report earnings more optimistically than the law allows, to keep up the price of its stock. Investigations began to find out just why it had hyped its results; the stock fell and matters appeared grave. But in 2000, under the leadership of Dennis Kozlowski, it beat back the SEC, acquired 40 more companies for a total of $9 billion, and earned very high profits. It became one of the darlings of Wall Street, with flattering profiles of its CEO appearing in *Business Week*, among other places. But all that money turned out to be irresistible; Kozlowski was caught raiding the company coffers ("grand larceny and enterprise corruption") for personal

---

[6]   Roben Farzad, "Jail Terms For 2 at Top of Adelphia," *The New York Times*, June 21, 2005, C1.

use – buying very expensive French masterpieces for his home (having them shipped to New Hampshire in order to avoid paying taxes on them), complementing the art with a $6,000 shower curtain for his bathroom, and finally throwing his wife a birthday bash largely at company expense on the island of Sardinia (replete with a statue of David in ice, spraying vodka from its penis) – to the tune of $600 million. Along with his CFO, Mark Swartz, he was convicted of misuse of company funds on June 17, 2005. On September 19, 2005, they were sentenced to 8 and one-third to 25 years in prison for the fraud.[7] Asked to comment, most of their peers said they got off easy.[8]

HealthSouth was at one point the country's largest provider of outpatient surgery, rehabilitation services, and diagnostic services, in over 1,800 facilities not only located in all 50 states but in Puerto Rico, Great Britain, Australia, and even Saudi Arabia. It was something of a byword in health care provision: in an industry where patient demands and expectations keep rising, Medicare and Medicaid reimbursement continues to contract, and employers are continually sifting through the competition to get the lowest costs for their medical insurance, Richard Scrushy and Health-South just seemed to be able to keep the costs down and post a profit quarter after quarter. The business press adored Scrushy, Newt Gingrich at one point wanted him to run for Congress, others thought he'd make a good governor of Alabama. In 1997 Scrushy took home $106 million, and he was only 45 years old.

---

[7] Andrew Ross Sorkin, "Ex-Tyco Officers Get 8 to 25 Years: 2 Sentenced in Crackdown on White-Collar Crime," *The New York Times*, September 20, 2005, A1, C4.
[8] Floyd Norris, "Why His Peers Say Kozlowski Got Off Easy," *The New York Times*, September 23, 2005, C1.

But it all turned out not to be true. It seems the popular CEO had overstated earnings and assets, year by year from 1999 on, in order to keep the price of the stock high enough to meet Wall Street expectations. He had cheated the investors, and the SEC launched an investigation. Worse, from the taxpayer's perspective, HealthSouth had apparently submitted claims, some estimated hundreds of thousands of claims, to Medicare and Medicaid for services that just weren't performed, or not as the claim said they had been performed. Worse yet, from the patient's perspective, the patients were not getting all the treatments they were supposed to get. If HealthSouth's medical quality matched its accounting quality, the patients were probably not harmed by the failure – at least the doctors didn't get a chance to make them worse – but it was still fraud. Pressured from three angles – investors, government insurers, and customers – HealthSouth had defrauded them all. On June 9, 2005, HealthSouth agreed to pay $100 million over a 2-year period to settle shareholder claims.

Scrushy was widely accused of personally directing the fraud, instructing subordinates to "fix" the numbers. He was put on trial in the same month the settlement was agreed upon, and prosecutors hoped for a resounding message-sending verdict. But on June 28, 2005, an Alabaman jury found him not guilty, sending shock waves through the entire prosecutorial effort.[9] What had happened? Recall the parable of the dishonest steward, told in the Gospel according to Luke, chapter 16: knowing he was about to be fired for dishonesty, the steward used his remaining time and power to forgive all manner of debts owed to his master, in this

[9]   Simon Romero and Kyle Whitmire, "Former Chief of HealthSouth Acquitted in $2.7 Billion Fraud," *The New York Times*, June 29, 2005, A1, C3.

way buying favor all through the community for when he needed help, which would be soon. We sometimes forget that rich men have many opportunities to endear themselves to the people who will sit on a local jury; Scrushy was very good at it. When he went on trial, he was the local boy who had made good, and who now led TV Bible classes. The jury chose to believe him rather than his (admittedly sleazy) associates, who had testified against him.[10] Annoyed, the shareholders took him to court on civil charges, and managed to wring $47.8 million out of his overstuffed bank accounts.[11] (The SEC had threatened as much, and may still act on its own.)[12] The controversy continues as I write.

There were many others. Why?

Choosing a Path in the Woods

We may start the reflection right here: What trails can we discern linking these stories? Where do they seem to go? Can we discern their origins, and project their further courses, in some way that will be profitable to us in our efforts to make sure that this *never happens again*?

A difficulty besets our discernment, which I choose to turn into an advantage: we can find *many* trails that thread through the woods of confusion in these cases, all of which carry promise

[10]   Kyle Whitmire, "Jurors Doubted Scrushy's Colleagues," *The New York Times*, July 2, 2005, C5.

[11]   Kyle Whitmire, "Judge Orders Ex-HealthSouth Chief to Repay Nearly $48 Million," *The New York Times*, January 4, 2006, C3.

[12]   "S.E.C. Set to Press Civil Case Against Scrushy," *The New York Times*, July 6, 2005, C5.

of enlightenment if followed. My problem is worse than that faced by Robert Frost, who found that "two paths diverged in a wood," and ended by taking the path "less traveled by." For I have many paths, charging off in different directions. I have a choice. I can try to do justice to all of them, mapping all the trails, completing (in the year 2075) a work the size of the Encyclopedia Britannica, or I can choose to be what some of my colleagues would call "simplistic": picking the explanation I think fits the stories best and arguing for it, and for the remedies it suggests, ignoring the complexities introduced by all the other considerations. If I do that, I will have to leave most of the paths to "another day," as Frost hoped, or more likely to other people, and choose only one of them to follow. *Unless* I do that, we will be here in this text for the rest of our lives. Fortunately, as above, many of the trails have been energetically trampled clear by enthusiastic hikers other than myself, many of whom will be found in the Bibliography; I am free to follow that path less traveled by, the path of personal growth, personal character, and personal decision, the proper province of the ethicist.

For a quick peek at the last page, let me summarize where my single simple trail will lead: I believe the fundamental error was made when our culture, the culture of the West, embraced Liberalism. "Liberalism" has meant many things in recent history, the most accepted meaning encompassing all of the protective measures for the poor that have always been associated with the extended family of tribal society – an odd closing of the circle of time. I choose to use the traditional meaning of Liberalism, arising from the Enlightenment in Western Europe. Liberalism, on my very traditional reading, rests on the thesis that in general, adults should be allowed to follow their desires wherever they lead, including the desire for accumulation of wealth beyond all reason, without limit and without social sanction. This notion of Liberalism, no other, grounds the entirety of the Free Market economy and the entirety of the political structure of legally guaranteed liberties and protections. Soon enshrined in law as a plague of "rights," the liberties so granted excluded almost every prohibition except those against personal assault and theft of property. The liberal creed read that Liberty should protect every act of every person, just so long as the act hurt no one else – that is, hurt no one in violation of law.

Economic hurt, for example, the harm that results if your business fails and you are left with debts, or if your job is terminated and you have no work to do, is excluded from the list of punishable hurts. Such hurts proceed from the ordinary workings of the free market (like the hurt that proceeds from the consumers deciding that they like the products offered for sale in the shop next to you more than they like yours), therefore it is not harm, so no one should be held responsible for it, unless some breach of duty can be found; and now you know why our courts of law are so terribly crowded – we can only treat the breach of duty, we cannot treat the hurt. Liberalism ultimately destroyed what I will call the Village: the natural human community that placed limits on human vice by the simple mechanism of transparency and moral consistency, and that destruction precipitated the scandals we live with today. I will argue that when we embraced Liberalism (represented by John Locke, Adam Smith, and the Utilitarians, over the strenuous objections of Conservatives like Edmund Burke), we adopted the ideal of a life without limits; and that loss of a sense of limit, of proportion, of natural ends, natural boundaries in human life, is the nerve of the vice that undermines our economics, our politics, and every one of our enterprises, public and private. In that embrace, we abandoned our communities, renounced our plain duty to care for each other and for the earth, and set our societies on the road to perdition. The abuses briefly chronicled above, which will forever go by the name of "Enron," follow immediately from that abandonment. That is the trail I will follow.

Before we go that way, though, let's take a very brief look at the others, for they all have something to contribute to the general discussion, you might want to follow them up yourself, and it will save time later if I don't have to explain why I am not following up this or that lead. We will consider the trails according to the occupational descriptions of their devoted guides – not a standard classification, to be sure, but useful in this case.

Business analysts (and the teachers of business students) have had a field day with the unhappy results of the latest round of corruption in the board room. (The best example of this literature is Kurt Eichenwald's *Conspiracy of Fools*, an account of the Enron debacle, and there are many others.) Everywhere they see mistakes, careless miscalculations, and ignorance of the fundamental truths of business enterprise. This direction, at least, is clear: if incompetence is the origin, and more of the same is the direction, then we have a solution: we need more and better technical education, primarily in our business schools, for business competence, for more thorough mastery of the fundamentals of business. I appreciate the force of this analysis; there was a good deal of sheer incompetence, and Enron's businesses (for example) never really made money.

But there was so much of it! How, in the late twentieth century, in administrations as favorable to business as we have ever had, could we get this positive epidemic of incompetence – from the best educated corporate officers in the world – amounting to systematic forgetfulness of the fundamentals of their trade, as

Eichenwald would have it? Can we reduce all this malfeasance to stupidity compounded by panic? But if that's our conclusion, where are we going to find "better educated" businessmen than these graduates of Wharton and Harvard? There has to be something more here, something more fundamental, that the business analysts, convinced that the market must always work if we will just follow the rules of rational self-interest, just cannot see. Part of the problem, I will argue, lies in the Enlightenment assumption that rational self-interest is rational, or generally represents the real interests of the individual or the society. We will have to take a better look at that assumption.

Social philosophers of Marxist background, with a consciousness of the problems of the market system honed from European schools of economics, have incorporated what they take to be the sad lessons of Enron into their social and political philosophy classes. For those of a socialist turn, these collapses indicate the faults of the market system, and the poison of the popular adoration of the false gods of capital, "free enterprise," and "liberty to accumulate wealth." When the market is allowed to run wild, this is the result: ordinary citizens are cheated out of their savings while the capitalists take home millions, as the value of their shares rises. Wall Street insists that profits must go up every year, every quarter. If they do not, investment analysts will downgrade your stock, it will decline in value, and you will be vulnerable to takeover. Wall Street and the Market are to blame; reappropriation of the resources of the country by the people is the answer; we need a fundamental restructuring of law and economy to reflect real needs and interests of the people. Enron and all the others are good arguments to abandon the "free market" altogether, but failing that, to reestablish very firm controls on its profit-seeking activities.

There is much that is appealing in this approach – certainly the spectacles that crowd our courts and our newspapers cause "the market" to give off such a stench that we might be forgiven for thinking it dead. But again, the social philosophers have picked as their target a framework constructed of human decisions and actions, while the source and grounds of those decisions and acts are precisely the problem. It is possible to be an honest business person; it is possible to run a company honestly, and fairly, taking into account the interests of all the stakeholders. The Market does not have to die. Business is not by definition exploitive and dishonest. Under what conditions can it run well?

Between the social philosophers and the defenders of the free market are the **regulators**, who value the free market but understand that it cannot function honestly without strict government oversight. When they say that business really needs regulatory oversight, they have a theoretical argument in their favor as well as a (very well confirmed) practical observation. For the obligation of a corporation, publicly owned, is to increase shareholder wealth; that part seems to be well understood. It need not do so in a dishonest way, but whatever means will increase wealth within the law, the law in force at any time, the corporation will adopt. Then if there are profitable actions that we do not wish the corporation to take, we *must* pass a law forbidding them, for whatever is not *forbidden*, in this field, is not *permitted* (the usual opposition), but *obligatory*. It's our job as a public to construct a rigid framework of law that will restrain all businesses from all evil. And when we find corruption, the regulators are convinced that just a few more good laws are needed, and repair immediately to the legislature, whence issues **Sarbanes-Oxley**, for instance.

It is surely true that in a complex economy, the free market at its best and most honest cannot operate well without regulation; but when it is far from its best, as in the current cases, using legislation to stem this tide of criminality is like trying to contain the rupture of a major water main by putting little dikes in front of the main streams. First of all, we're not getting at the source of the problem, so it will continue, requiring ever more dikes, and second, even the dikes we have will not work: the water, and the criminals, will simply find their way around them. They're much smarter than we are. Laws only work when the people are law-abiding; laws to regulate large corporations only work when the managers of those corporations are law-abiding, and these just were not. There is also the possibility, which we will revive at the end, that really good people don't need every action dictated by law to be good. We may hold that out as a hope.

We are brought back to the individuals, the people who made these decisions, and must surely have known, at some level, that they were wrong. For philosophers of a more reflective turn, **ethicists** who meditate on all human conduct, Enron represents a serious failure of fundamental morality. It is not that their companies did not, officially, adhere to the highest ethical values. Enron's Code of Ethics, over 60 pages in length, was a model of its kind; Tyco International avows itself committed to the highest standards of integrity. Somehow, the individuals who were bound by those standards simply failed to meet them. Yet they did not seem to be, at the beginning, truly bad people by nature, and they had had every educational advantage. Surely they understood the standards they were expected to meet. What made them "go bad," what made them indulge in astoundingly greedy and criminal behavior? Are there ways that such going bad can be prevented, or stopped before it reaches these terrible ends? Will this trail, the trail of personal ethics and character, yield any solution at all? No wonder the others have avoided it; we will pursue it.

For I think the general public deserves better than it has got out of these scandals. Besides being the dupe, the mark for these con men, the ultimate losers, as their pension funds are compromised and their share of the tax burden increased by the cheating of the very wealthy, the public is left with only a media circus to cover a massive fraud with few means of understanding it. For the public, there is only titillation, and wonder, and, if the public is at all thoughtful, despair. Here were the most privileged creatures on the face of the earth, born into solid families in the wealthiest country in the world, with the best college and graduate educations, fortunate to work for unbelievably high salaries for some of the best companies on the globe, philanthropists, the company names on community projects, exactly the men and women that we would have expected to be our leaders in the new century – and look, they were up to their armpits in filth, lying, cheating, and stealing. What motivation could possibly have led them to risk their great good fortune for so little more money and the risk of lifelong disgrace? What depth of moral corruption explains the betrayal of the nation's trust by those who profited most from the system that grounds that trust?

In what follows, we will try to put the scandals in a larger context – in fact, in the largest context possible, the entirety of human nature. For it is not just business enterprise that has wandered off its moral tracks. Education, church, statecraft, and God's green earth itself are equally at risk, threatened by neglect, by chicanery, by exploitation and diversion from mission by powerful and greedy agencies.

We were put on this earth to take care of the earth and to take care of each other, and frankly, we're doing a very bad job of both.

We will have to rediscover the responsibilities of our stewardship before the mess will be cleaned up, and those responsibilities extend well beyond economics. In order to do that, we are going to have to recreate the context of morality in which our race came to moral consciousness. Ultimately, the answer to that "why" question, with regard to Enron and all the others, is that in the development of our advanced economies we have put some human beings into contexts where humans have little practice working, and where normal controls are gone, and the results that we have seen are grimly predictable. Let us see how that might be so.

1

The World, the Flesh, and the Devil

A Look in the Mirror is Not Reassuring

It is always tempting to blame "the system," whatever the system may be, for corporate collapse. What on earth might "the system" be, in this case? The modern corporation? Wall Street and the Stock Market? Free Enterprise? The answer will turn out to be all and none of the above. We start with the prime insight: it isn't the system that cheats; it is the people. People do crimes, not systems. Systems do not lie, cheat, and steal; people do. But beyond that, the system in which the crimes were committed was no accident of history. It was deliberately shaped by some of the people who most profited from the crimes they committed, in order that their behavior would not be criminal (or at least not as criminal as it would have been under the old system). So the offenders are to blame, not only for their behavior within the system, but for the constructing of the system itself.

We will need to look at the people, not as individuals, but as players in a system that they had helped to create. We will not look at the offenders as individuals because their past tells us nothing, or at least nothing helpful: they were good Americans, they were raised by good families in good schools, they had, all of them, an unbroken history of well-earned success. They were good people, as far as we can tell, until the events that brought them to court and to the pages of *The New York Times* (beyond adulatory mentions in the Business section). But they had helped to change the system in a way that made it possible for any potential they might have to commit crimes to be realized. It is not so implausible that good and well-educated people, given the opportunity by a particularly advantageous system, should commit these crimes. There are troubling potentials for crimes, even unspeakable crimes, in most people – possibly all of us. There are historic views of humans as inevitably prone to crime, tainted with sin, which look very intelligent in the light of current affairs. The root of the problem is the human being, and it looks from here like the human is rotten.

An Ancient Fable Says It All

Consider the tales of two rings. The first is from the Northern myth cycle, which shows up as the One Ring of Power in J. R. R. Tolkien's *Lord of the Rings*,[1] Isildur's Bane, derived from the Germanic Ring of the Nibelungen, that made its wearer invisible, and through demonic power, gave the bearer enormous power that, tragically, he could never use for good. Through the

[1]   J. R. R. Tolkien, *The Lord of the Rings*, many editions; see London: Folio Society, 1977.

character Boromir, Tolkien considers the possibility that the Ring, now found, might be used to defeat the enemy, Sauron, the Devil. The leader of the Elves, Elrond, gives the answer that captures the Northern tradition exactly:

> "Alas, no," said Elrond. "We cannot use the Ruling Ring. That we now know too well. It belongs to Sauron and was made by him alone, and is altogether evil. Its strength, Boromir, is too great for anyone to wield at will, save only those who had already a great power of their own. But for them it holds an even deadlier peril. The very desire of it corrupts the heart. Consider Saruman [a Wizard who had been turned to the Dark Side]. If any of the Wise should with this Ring overthrow the Lord of Mordor, using his own arts, he would then set himself on Sauron's throne, and yet another Dark Lord would appear. And that is another reason why the Ring should be destroyed: as long as it is in the world it will be a danger even to the Wise. For nothing is evil in the beginning. Even Sauron was not so. I fear to take the Ring to hide it. I will not take the Ring to wield it."[2]

Is this the Ring that we should fear? Can demonic power alone account for all evil? Quite possibly, but our tradition has a more likely story, and a more available Ring, in the Southern myth cycle, centering on the Greek and Roman gods. Its story is that of Gyges, from Plato's *Republic*. Let Plato tell the story:

> The story tells how he was a shepherd in the King's service. One day there was a great storm, and the ground where his flock was feeding was rent by an earthquake. Astonished at the sight, he went down into the chasm and saw, among other wonders of which the story tells, a brazen horse, hollow, with windows in

---

[2]   Ibid., vol. I, *The Fellowship of the Ring*, p. 307.

its sides. Peering in, he saw a dead body, which seemed to be of more than human size. It was naked save for a gold ring, which he took from the finger and made his way out. When the shepherds met, as they did every month, to send an account to the King of the state of his flocks, Gyges came wearing the ring. As he was sitting with the others, he happened to turn the bezel of the ring inside his hand. At once he became invisible, and his companions, to his surprise, began to speak of him as if he had left them. Then, as he was fingering the ring, he turned the bezel outwards and became visible again. With that, he set about testing the ring to see if it really had this power, and always with the same result: according as he turned the bezel inside or out he vanished and reappeared. After this discovery he contrived to be one of the messengers sent to the court. There he seduced the Queen, and with her help murdered the King and seized the throne.[3]

Plato continues:

Now suppose there were two such magic rings, and one were given to the just man, the other to the unjust. No one, it is commonly believed, would have such iron strength of mind as to stand fast in doing right or keep his hands off other men's goods, when he could go to the market-place and fearlessly help himself to anything he wanted, enter houses and sleep with any woman he chose, set prisoners free and kill men at his pleasure, and in a word go about among men with the powers of a god. He would behave no better than the other; both would take the same course.[4]

Underlying the story is a clear account of human nature, one that I find very plausible. The "point is that men practice

---

[3]   *The Republic of Plato*, ed. and tr. Francis MacDonald Cornford (Oxford: Oxford University Press, 1941), pp. 44–5.

[4]   Ibid.

[justice] against the grain, for lack of power to do wrong. . . . We shall catch the just man taking the same road as the unjust; he will be moved by self-interest, the end which it is natural to every creature to pursue as good, until forcibly turned aside by law and custom to respect the principle of equality."[5]

The story of Enron and Tyco may, of course, be a tale of demonic possession – Satan hiding in corporate jets? Or it may be just a tale of invisibility – anyone, with Gyges's ring, will behave disgracefully. We should be clear on which tale is told by these scandals. For if there are evil supernatural Rings lying around, filled with demonic power, presumably we should be very careful to avoid putting them on; fortunately, in this our real world, such Rings are not to be found. But Rings that do nothing more than make us invisible – offshore special purpose entities, Swiss banks, gated communities, and the general anonymity of the city – are everywhere we look, there for the purchase. And when we have them, like Gyges, we go for the money and the power. Who needs Satan? All the evil we need is built into our nature, and we are very well aware of it. Now, why? Is God, our Creator, playing some huge and horrible joke on us? It's a good question.

Lead Us Not Into Temptation

Where does our sinfulness, our violence and greed, come from? Let me start off this section with an explanation of method. I will argue that tendencies to violence and greed, as well as tendencies to cooperation, are *hardwired* in us. The metaphor, being contemporary, is well understood in its primary context: the

[5] Ibid.

physical structure of computers, for instance, permanently limits what those computers can do, and in respect to their hardware their operations cannot change, no matter what variety of software (programs) are put in them. Humans, too, have hardware: not just the muscles and bones of the species, but the underlying set of tendencies etched in the genes over tens of thousands of years of selection. Tendencies to selfish conduct are built into our genetic heritage, arising not from any genetic descent from other animals, but simply from the conditions of our own lives during the last 50,000 years of our history. Remember always that we are the children of the survivors, not of those who did not survive; we have been selected for sin. Simple natural selection, what used to be called "social Darwinism," explains the kind of bad behavior that has just plagued our business world.

We are not the first to use natural selection as an explanation, and the method raises a quick objection, which we will have to deal with first. It might be asked: So what? We know we have regrettable tendencies to (at least) seven deadly sins – Lust, Anger, Sloth, Vanity, Envy, Gluttony, and Avarice (they're easy to remember: just think LAS VEGAs, with the last "s" for "sin," and you'll have it), and we don't need genomic analysis to prove it. How does this "natural selection" account help our understanding? What is added to the observation – that humans often behave in antisocial ways – by the claim that we have somehow "inherited" a tendency to do so? The answer is twofold: *first*, the universal claim that all humans tend to greed and violence removes the aura of abnormality, deviation, from sinfulness. It denies our deep desire to pretend that the offenders in the dock were "bad apples," not like us at all. Whether or not we choose to admit it, all the tendencies that led these privileged executives to abuse the trust placed in them, are present in us also. Their

24

situation is universal. *Second*, it warns us that there will not be any institutional modification that will wipe out these tendencies. We will not "learn the lessons" of Enron, any more than we learned the lessons of Watergate, or Auschwitz, or the War to End Wars, which didn't. Our corporations, like our government, will continue to be secretive, rapacious and corrupt, unless stopped in each generation by the good sense and vigilance of the people. And they can be stopped; that's the good news. But not by pretending that violence, physical and otherwise, does not exist, or that we have somehow outgrown greed.

Sinfulness, according to our tradition, has three main sources – the World, the Flesh, and the Devil. What do these mean? We'll take them slightly out of order:

The first source to consider is the Devil, only in order to dismiss it. There is a tradition that Satan himself intervenes in our lives to distract us from the truth, to tempt us with riches and power and magical abilities (consider the temptations of Jesus in the desert) and generally works to disrupt our relationship with God. In the Northern tradition of the Ring, above, the Ring of Richard Wagner and J. R. R. Tolkien, it is the Devil, or evil, or Sauron, or heaven knows what other demonic spirit, that inhabits the ring, and those who succumb to the temptation to wear it inevitably end up ruled by that devil. Innocent life, human, or possibly hobbit, powerless against the force of measureless evil, is in that way captured and made to share in the guilty evil of the evil spirits, the Spirits of the Air. It's an attractive hypothesis; it lets us believe that we are innocent from the cradle, and only become evil through traffic with something supernatural. (As a matter of fact, that's what Elrond says, in the passage above.) Maybe, it follows, some special talisman or prayer or pact with a saint will keep me from all evil? Infinite superstition follows, and this is always fun, but for the purposes of this essay, we intend to disregard the hypothesis. It is outside the scope of the work and, frankly, outside the scope of any intelligent discussion in the field of ethics. Whatever pleas may be accepted by the judge as the offenders come to trial, "the Devil made me do it" will not be on the list of those acceptable.

The others are more interesting. "The Flesh," in the traditional trilogy of temptations, is essentially appetite or desire, not for money, which is only symbolic and has nothing essentially to do with flesh, but for things that taste good, feel good, and generally satisfy the physical desires that come with having a body. St. Augustine singled out "lust," sexual desire, as the quintessential heart of sin. It is part of the normal and healthy rhythm of life, and without it there would be no children, but it can spiral out of control, as Augustine knew, and as every student of human nature since Augustine has known well, and when it does, it destroys lives and wrecks the very families it created. "The world," in this understanding, is the world of human society, families and churches, employers, getting and spending, governing, educating, playing games and fighting wars – anything we do in structured groups. The human world is composed of practices, institutions, rule-governed activities through which we interact in any activity larger than the immediate family. These structures systematically reward practice-supporting behavior and systematically punish behavior that deviates from their norms. For Gyges, the institutional rewards of wealth and political power were all the temptation he needed, and he became a very sinful man indeed. Plato and all other traditional moral teachers[6] were

---

[6] Consider the same trilogy, again in slightly different order, as the evils that must be renounced by a candidate for baptism; see *The Book of Common Prayer* 1979 edition, p. 302.

acutely aware of the extent of the destruction that these institutions might cause. But then, why do we have them?

Let's start with the flesh. We should not forget that we are animals – flesh and blood, born and mortal, arriving in this world with the dual agenda of survival and reproduction hardwired in every nerve and muscle. That agenda requires us to seek out, and succumb to, occasions of the sins of the Flesh – the animal who takes every opportunity to eat and to copulate is more likely to survive and to leave offspring than the one that does not, and since the tendency to seek and take such opportunities is at least in part genetically determined, that tendency will be reinforced in subsequent generations. We are the children of the survivors, recall, so we have the same tendency; that is all we mean by "hardwired," and that part, at least, is simple.

We are also social animals, who satisfy our animal needs in a structure of group (herd, community) acceptability. As Aristotle insisted, outside of human society, the human who survives at all does so as a beast (unless he's some sort of misplaced god); only within human society, structured in some human way, can he be human. But that means that tendencies to indulge in the sins of the World are also hardwired, inherent in and essential to human nature.

Consider: In the uncertain social currents of foraging life, survival was not assured. When the strong survived and the weak did not, those who seized resources and power (or allied themselves with those who had seized resources and power) had the best chance to assure their own survival and the survival of their families (that is, of their genetic line). Behavior in conformity with the rule, "seize what you can when you can and keep it," is observable on a daily basis; there were occasions, fortunately rare at present, when it was the only behavior that would keep you alive.

There is (possibly as a consequence of that last?) a sense in which that rule embodies a particularly primitive, but attractive, ideal of masculinity; survival is the first imperative, and the survivor is admired. (Consider the popularity of the "reality TV" show of that name.) The parallel ideal of femininity, incorporating the behavior most likely to keep a woman's genes in the population, is one of attachment to the powerful; as the male seeks to dominate, the female seeks to attach herself to the dominant male who will protect her and her offspring. As a survival strategy for a social animal, this imperative generalizes easily to mixed populations: "in uncertainty, find a powerful person and attach yourself to him, trading service for protection." How does all this amateur anthropology explain Enron? When the people with whom you associate have been publicly identified as the smartest, the most forward-looking, the richest and most powerful people in the country – Masters of the Universe – the decision to join yourself to them, and to do what will keep you under their protection, is blessed by your genes. It feels comfortable, very comfortable.

Our associative talents go well beyond power-seeking and power-serving. As far back as we can find in human experience, human associations have displayed a rich variety, running through all the traditional forms of government (autocracy, oligarchy, democracy, hereditary aristocracy) and cultural arrangements. In the travels and changing circumstances of the formative millennia of human existence, survival has been furthered more by adaptability to new circumstances, by a keen set of antennae that read social imperatives, than by the ability to use violence – the use of violence, as a matter of fact, is counterproductive, even suicidal, in the majority of encounters with new situations. An ability to read the new social situation quickly, figure out what behavior is demanded, what rewarded and what punished, has always been and remains a key survival value. Rapid adjustment to a new group's agenda is the only route to ensure that acceptance in the group and maximize the possibility that the group will make it possible to satisfy primary needs of survival and reproduction. The ordinary price paid for such support is group loyalty: whatever enemies the group may have now become the enemies of the new member. When we say that people are social animals, we mean no more than that we have to satisfy our primary needs in structured groups; put more simply, humans are obligatory team players. We are the children of the successful ones.

What kind of human being do we see in all this? We see a creature with a predictable set of survival-oriented tendencies inherited from tens of thousands of years of life on this earth, and the tendencies conflict. In a new and potentially threatening situation, he can fight, run away, or fit in, but he cannot do all of them at once. Social cues, read quickly and (probably) unconsciously, will have to tell him what course of action to follow. Whatever strategy is adopted, the alternatives lie close to the surface, ready to be mobilized if the same unconscious reading now suggests that a better course is possible. We are not a collection of Selfish Genes; we are a nuanced collection of potentials, activated by social cues, and the social cues are embedded in our cultures.

Turning from the individual to the group beyond the family – the tribe, village, nation – we see that its interest depends very much on helping the individual make that choice in favor of fitting in to the group's agenda. Random violence, appropriation of resources, assaults on women, will destroy all that the group has built, not only by the damage done by the violent offender, but even more by the instantly aroused tendencies to violent revenge of all of the others in the group. (This is why the first laws restraining violence restrained not the offender but the avenger of blood.) All of our social institutions evolved from that time have been at the service of restraining and ordering violence, greed and the hardwired lust for power, and the survival of the higher orders of society depends on the success of those institutions. To the most successful of them we now turn.

The Village

The longest lasting of these institutions we may call the "village": the hereditary group, bonded by kinship, membership in which is lifelong (or obtained only after long residence), in full view of which we grow, apprentice, marry, practice our trade, have our children, raise them, retire and die. Conscience, literally "knowing together," is formed and reinforced on a daily basis in the village. Since everything takes place in the village, everything we do is seen and monitored by the village; we are never outside its purview. Even the formally "invisible" realm of village life is also "seen," for religion, the church, is the product and extension of the village. Neighbors and God adopt similar roles of support and monitoring; God holds you in view when the village is not physically watching. Privacy, idiosyncrasy, is a morally dubious condition all by itself, in the view of the village. What, after all, do you have to hide? Whether we speak of a tribal village in Africa, unchanged for 60,000 years, or a small town in the American Midwest, village structures have the same function: to protect the members from external harm, to accommodate their means of making a living, and to reinforce the strong bonds that make human survival and reproduction possible – through rituals of initiation, maturity, marriage, and death. In the village all is shared; as in the family from which it arose, except in very, *very*, special circumstances, no one is allowed to starve, or be idle, to prey on the others or be a victim of predation. Everyone is important, and will be taken care of if need arises, even if grudgingly.

Note that the relation between the individual and the Village is not one of opposition, although there are certainly times when the individual would like to do something that the village prevents. The individual is the product of the village, raised up by it to perform some traditional function, encouraged, shaped, and defined by the nurturing society. The life of the individual is an essential part of the collective life of the village, as the village's rhythms are part of each member's life at all times. While the village is at peace and functioning well, the individual may hardly notice its role as restrainer of impulses of which he may be hardly aware.

Where does the village come from? The village arose, on the sketchy accounts of the anthropologists (and the systematic, but hardly historical, account given by Aristotle in the *Politics*) from the nomadic extended families in which we lived for several million years. When humans became sedentary (which some groups were able to do even before the discovery of agriculture), the human groups began to accumulate material goods (imposs-ible in a nomadic existence) and to enjoy leisure – the evenings around the fire – in which the first stories of men and gods were told, and the tribal culture was born. The spine of the culture was the tribal *narrative*, the story of the creation of the world, the origins of the tribe, and the initial acts of the gods, giving the law, punishing and rewarding, winning mighty battles for the tribe, consecrating the land. Somewhere on that land the gods lived still, watching over their people. We all lived in villages (or stayed in nomadic family groups) until about 6,000 years ago, when the first cities were born and the possibility of a truly anonymous existence in a pluralistic society arose.

It is important to Aristotle's account, and to this one, that the village is self-sufficient, at least economically. (For a full political life, a larger and more varied association is needed; since it is in that larger association that all regulation will have to originate, we'll come back to it presently.) Every economic transaction, every trade, manufacture, purchase or sale, begins and ends in the village. That means that every selfish appropriation of more than one's share, every corner cut, every shady deal that enriches the dealer, hurts someone close by. In general, humans know when they have been hurt, at least if it keeps happening. They tend to avoid occasions of hurt, and that includes avoiding merchants that cheat them. Honesty is indeed the best policy in the village, in fact it is the only policy; the trader, dealer, or craftsman who cannot inspire the trust of his neighbors, by quality craftsmanship and honest dealing, will soon be out of business. This village is part of our recent past in the United States; Benjamin Franklin's *Poore Richard's Almanack*, preaching industry, honesty, and prudence in business and simplicity of life, is its manifesto.

What does the village have to do with Dennis Kozlowski? Well, had he had to carry out his illegal dealings in a village where everyone knew pretty much what he was doing, he would not have got away with it. The $6,000 shower curtain would have been noticed and condemned. That's the least important part of it. More importantly, if he had been part of that village from birth, and knew that the people hurt by his thefts were the people he relied on to rescue him when he ran into a patch of bad luck, it might not have occurred to him to start his scams at all. The village is the source of moral behavior from the beginning. It seems that we have always known that human integrity, like human altruism, all on its own, cannot take very much pressure and cannot be depended on to get much done. We have relied on the village – on God, parents, teachers, cops, neighbors – society in general – to keep our neighbors in line so they cannot harm us, and incidentally to keep us away from situations where we know we will do wrong.

How Bad Can It Get? The Unspeakable Crimes of the Very Good

All of which brings us, not only to the Crime in the Suites, the wholesale looting of American enterprise, but further, to Abu Ghraib, Guantánamo, and the other recent horrors from the War against Terrorism. Well-raised boys tortured detainees to death, detainees they knew were probably innocent. Well-raised girls participated in rituals of sexual humiliation, taunted naked Arab men, played with their helplessness, then made sure that amateur photography recorded the atrocities, then sent the pictures around on the Internet. Was it a repeat of Auschwitz? No; but by the time Auschwitz happened in occupied Poland in the 1940s, the Village of the Third Reich had become one nationwide cult of hatred and dedication to national conquest. The young men who casually slaughtered Jews all over Eastern Europe had been raised to do that, or at least to cultivate the feelings that would make such acts possible and even enjoyable. But the young men (and women) of the American facilities in Iraq, Afghanistan, and Guantánamo Bay were raised by good God-fearing families in the United States, supporting no ethic of hatred or contempt, schooled in tolerance and appreciation for other cultures, taught to obey rules and to harm no one. Now suddenly, no more than a year away from their families, they were engaged in acts of sexual abuse that they would not have dared to think about at home.

Wherever sin is anonymous, it abounds, without limit. One of the stranger phenomena of contemporary life is the explosion of anonymous sex. Prostitutes always hung out in the less fashionable parts of town, so as not to be seen by the better sort, and the johns never gave their names; but they at least had to leave home for sex out of sight of family and neighbors. No longer. In the deregulatory 1980s (see below), a business called "sex-chat" blossomed over the phone lines (the infamous "1–900" numbers). In an article on offshore gambling, business writer Kurt Eichenwald describes a family pornography business, where the daughter of the founder, Ruth Parasol,

> emerged as one of the small clique of prominent executives in the growing world of interactive pornography. . . . Ms Parasol and her father established Starlink Communications, another phone-sex business. They also invested with [Seth] Warshavsky's biggest venture ever, the Internet Entertainment Group. Cash was coming in by the fistful for everyone. While online pet stores and cosmetics companies were struggling, Internet pornography was a gold mine. The phone lines almost printed money, and, through I.E.G., Mr. Warshavsky became the most prominent businessman in online pornography, with hundreds of thousands of paying members . . . [7]

---

[7]   Kurt Eichenwald, "At PartyGaming, Everything's Wild," *The New York Times*, June 26, 2005, first Business page (section 3, p. 1).

Hundreds of thousands? All that is required is anonymity, for hundreds of thousands of men (mostly) to spend hours in expensive occupations that they themselves probably regard as disgraceful, and would never dare to describe to their families and neighbors.

We don't have to go to war or the phone lines to find examples of "good boys gone bad," or girls, for that matter. Sex offenders are often the folks next door, with good jobs and clean records, who are presented with a temptation, and an opportunity, that have never come together before in their lives, and suddenly they begin doing things that their neighbors, when they find out about them, can hardly believe. Confronted with their own acts when reality has reasserted itself, sometimes the offenders themselves find it difficult to believe what they have done. What had happened? Their acts were anonymous and invisible; no one was watching, no one knew, no one had the chance to comment – and so the fantasies went wild, and morality was forgotten. The Internet, otherwise known as Anonymity.com, has created whole new categories of sexual predation that would have been impossible even a quarter of a century ago. When the cops – inner, outer, official or not – can't watch us, what do we do? Unbelievably bad stuff, it appears. The people who did these things were not bad people to start with. To commit terrible crimes, all you need is freedom from the constraints of a village, of a community that cannot be escaped, and (sometimes) a few collaborators, in person or over the sex-chat phone, to reassure you that you're all right.

The Human Alone

Just below the surface, what are we, really? We have known all along that the individual human is never strong. The individual human is radically incomplete as a moral person. Alone, unwatched, not with others, invisible, anonymous, we do things we would never accept if we had to talk about them in public.

This is not the place to take on the whole of human sin, human evil. In this essay we are interested primarily in that little suburb of sin located in Enron, Adelphia, Tyco, WorldCom, and the others. There's enough evil in the heart of America's free market to keep us busy at least until this evening. But we need to know how the village failed, how business – not just one corporation, but the whole business community – went astray, and at the end, what we can do to restore morality to the corporate boardroom.

2

The Lethal Marriage of Ideology and Opportunity

The Pendulum Swings Right

Public life is a series of conflicts, and that is as it should be. Conflicts among occupational and cultural groups, to advance their interests, are the stuff of democratic politics; conflicts between the political parties that would organize those interests define government. But there is a larger conflict, the conflict between liberty and order, which underlies them all, and that is the conflict that needs adjudication now. In the vast "social contract" of human society, we need both liberty (entailing unpredictable change) and order (entailing stability of expectations). They are not incompatible; they are moments in a single process, and we need them both.

We need enough stability for the individual to grow, to learn to rely on a world in which unsupported objects *always* fall and stealing is *always* followed by a trip back to the store to return the stolen object and apologize. The regularity of reward and punishment, no less than the regularity of physical laws, is essential for a child to develop a sense of responsibility. The protection of the institutions of society is essential, in exactly the same way, for people to commit themselves to jobs that will take up the larger part of their time, strength, and energy until they have very little of those left. (Question for later: if they are willing to make such a commitment, does the employer who reaps the value of that commitment have a parallel obligation not to terminate that job?) The protection of the stable institutions is at least as necessary for people to commit themselves to marriage, and to raising a family; if weddings seem to be later and later in this society, sometimes lacking altogether, that may have something to do with the destabilizing of economic and cultural expectations. The individual needs stability, physical, economic and moral, and tends to become rootless and indecisive without it. Sometimes he never leaves his parents' home.

Individual liberty, on the other hand, is an absolute requirement for the society to survive. Circumstances change, and have always changed; necessary innovations, as most of us know, are rarely the product of committees or consensus. Individuals seeing a need, and striking out along an initially unpopular (certainly untraditional) path in order to meet it, are the only agents of necessary change. The society that locks up liberty is doomed. But the very innovations that the creative individual brings to pass, by flouting (or skirting) the institutions of the society, threaten or seem to threaten the stability that the other individuals need.

We may summarize the social contract:[1] we need enough stability for the individual to grow and flourish, and enough liberty for the society to adapt to change. It may be noted,

[1] With Robert Ardrey. See *The Social Contract: A Personal Inquiry into the Evolutionary Sources of Order and Disorder* (New York: Doubleday, 1971).

that the current rhetoric, dating from the nineteenth-century Romantics, that claims liberty as an individual right (and desire), while stability is the interest of society (and tyrants), has it just wrong. That particular error will haunt us through our attempts to make sense of the current scandals: for if the Romantic opposition is correct, if liberty is the cry of the individual, and stability that of the society, then as soon as "the society" has "decided" that individual liberty shall be allowed full room to prosper, there is no more argument for stability; if the individual and the society both cry for liberty, then we are in agreement. But of course, we are not. In the "decision," whatever its source, to allow the individual full unbridled liberty to pursue whatever the individual may want, we have loosed a demon among us; we have given Gyges permission to do anything he wants to do as long as he can stay invisible. That was really not a good idea.

After an unexpectedly profound rearrangement of national priorities in the 1960s, the United States spent the 1970s carrying them out: the implementation of a civil rights agenda institutionalizing rights for all races, new limits on a variety of corrupt corporate practices abroad, new limits on the rights of industries to carry on operations that pollute the environment, new limits on corporate secrecy, all coinciding with a rush of innovation in the arts, education, and relationships between the sexes. In this period, America became the wonder of the world in its new tolerance for differences and its responsible and forward-looking legislation in health care and environmental protection. But the change was significantly disruptive, and inevitably, established interests were crossed. In the proper order of things, change should be followed by reaction; in the inexorable swing of the political pendulum, we tire of the faults of one way of looking at our public life, and decide to adopt another. So the pendulum swung toward relaxing the restrictions on business and economic activity, while reining in the wild cultural experimentation that had characterized the "soaring sixties"; that was normal.

We say that the pendulum has swung toward the "right." "Right," in this context, needs some explaining, and this is as good a point as any to explain. What counts as "right" and "left" has something to do with the arrangement of the French *Parlement* during the French Revolution; in the seating arrangement in that legislative body, the traditionalists were to the right of some center point and the radicals to the left. By now that distinction is totally lost, and "right" and "left" have fallen into some disarray in contemporary politics. At this point in history, "Right" stands for political and cultural authoritarianism (protection of executive prerogative and legal limits on homosexual expression, for instance), and economic liberty; "Left" stands for political or cultural liberty (free speech, free press, protection of gay rights) and economic authoritarianism (enforcing transparency and accountability in both government and business). Those on the far "right" want to tell us who we can sleep with and what we can read, but demand complete freedom for the businessman to make a profit; those on the far "left" leave us free to marry anyone we want and think any way we want, but require all economic enterprise to conform to rules designed to promote what we see as the greatest good for the country as a whole. All others fall in between, somewhere; the positions as described, of course, are caricatures. In practical translation, the "business" community opts for positions on the right, and the "common good" initiatives come from the left. Note that both right and left seek to satisfy the social contract, protecting stable institutions for the security of the individual and allowing liberty for the sake of societal adaptation. The right provides stability and emotional security through enforcement of traditional cultural understandings on sex and religion, while allowing liberty on the economic side – they can defend against unsettling public displays of homosexuality but are helpless against layoffs. The left provides stability on the economic side while leaving culture free – they can promise protections against arbitrary job loss, but nerves-rattling cultural experiments are welcome. The public is responsible for choosing among them. The public chooses wisely, in general; when one impulse has gone far enough, they vote for the other. The inevitability of that alternation has given rise to the image of the "pendulum": it is a good thing that it swings. But notice that its latest swing is of very long duration and of very great consequence. In the next section we explore that consequence.

Free Market Liberalism and Village Conservatism

To find the origins of the present disease, we will have to make a short expedition back to the origins of the Liberalism that underlies the free market. "Liberalism," villain of the plot in my writing of the story, began in an age of enlightenment as a reaction against a stultified world of hardened traditions and community constraints that surely appeared useless to the best thinkers of the age. Adam Smith's *Wealth of Nations*, at the heart of the new movement, adopted the philosophical orientation of Utilitarianism, advanced by Smith's contemporary Jeremy Bentham. Utilitarianism's signature innovation, in which liberal economics joins, was to view the Individual, not the Community, as the primitive quantity in all morals and policy. The rational individual, conceiving desires out of his own individual experience of pleasure and pain, measures the value of every act and every thing according to its tendency to produce pleasure or pain for himself or herself; the collective good, then, is nothing other than the goods of all the individuals under consideration, added up. A "felicific calculus," a calculus for measuring happiness, was developed so that individual and collective pleasures and pains could be precisely stated and precisely measured; the result of this scientific calculation, the sum when you have added the pleasures and subtracted the pains, tells you the best of the alternatives available to the individual or to the policymaker. At no point does the "collective," the community, emerge with rights, interests, or even an existence, of its own.

Bentham did not take on the economic implications of his ethical theory, or of the understanding of human nature that grounds it; that was left to Adam Smith. But the search for personal wealth was no part of Adam Smith's vision, either. In his previous book, *The Theory of Moral Sentiments*, he had argued that the acquisition of money was a mistake, undertaken in the vain hope that personal display would translate into community respect. (He acknowledged, however, the usefulness of trade in useless trinkets to advance the interests of the nation.) He had no love for the wealthy, and regarded the secondary level of economy – the bankers, stockbrokers, insurers, and the like – with a healthy suspicion. But he set the individualized, atomized, selfish model of humanity and economy squarely in the middle of Western thought, and there it has stayed, even after economist David Ricardo, some 40 years later, demonstrated that capitalism must inevitably result in perpetual class conflict. (A young Hegelian, Karl Marx, found that conclusion very interesting and proceeded to draw his own conclusions on its implications. But that's another book.) Still, Smith's theory, and Ricardo's extension, focused on the wealth of the nation, not the individual; the cult of individual wealth did not begin until later in the century. (An interesting interpretation of that cult – with curious contemporary overtones – has it the product of the evangelical Christianity of the mid-nineteenth century, which preached that in God's providential world, great wealth was a sign of God's favor.[2])

Smith and all the other proponents of the Enlightenment, the new rational liberalism, were not unopposed. They were opposed by conservatives, who did little writing about what they believed, for obvious reasons: "conservatism" has no existence until there is a "liberalism" to challenge the existing order, which conservatism will defend. So conservatism has no theory of its own – its initial impulse is to defend whatever is being challenged, which means that it proceeds from an implied premise that "whatever is, is good," which its proponents probably don't believe. Edmund Burke, who in his *Reflections on the Revolution in France* opposed the liberalism of the rationalists who had supplied the theoretical revolutionary basis for the French Revolution, took pride in the fact that he had no abstract theory to impose on society. The institutions that had evolved in each country, he guessed, were probably right for that country, as expressing the collective wisdom of thousands of small decisions made over the centuries, tried out and kept if they worked, discarded if they did not. The very embeddedness of institutions, changed only when the changes seem to have happened on the ground without the additions of any ideas at all, justifies their continuation.

Nevertheless, we can extract a theory, conservative theory, from the writings of Burke and Aristotle, in the light thrown by the first chapter's considerations of human evil. It might be worth

[2]   Gordon Bigelow, "Let There Be Markets: The Evangelical Roots of Economics," *Harper's Magazine*, May 2005, pp. 33–8.

the time to make a quick sketch of this theory, if only to ground the conclusions of the next chapter. (Those who do not enjoy theory are encouraged to skip the next section.)

The Origins of the Moral Human

If Smith originates his Self-Centered Human in the Market, conservatism will originate a Community-Centered Human back in the Village.[3] On the liberal orientation to political philosophy, the *natural* human – empirical man, "man in the state of nature," the human being as we happen to find him – is fully equipped with the characteristics needed to participate in the moral life. Our desires, aversions, interests, and rights are inalienably a part of us. (Whether the rights or the desires take priority is a matter for dispute; liberals disagree.) The *good society* is defined in terms of natural humanity: the society that best satisfies those desires and protects those rights is the good society. And from society in turn, the notion of a *good person* is derived: a good person is one who serves that society, respecting the rights of others and serving the interests of others, as prescribed by that society. On the conservative orientation, the line of derivation is the same, but it runs in the opposite direction. The primary concept for the conservative is the *good person*, the mature person who possesses to the fullest the most characteristically human traits, who is just what a human being should be – the fully realized person. The

[3]   What follows is essentially from Aristotle, from the *Politics* and the *Nicomachean Ethics*. I claim no originality. I have, however, summarized the conclusions of this reflection before, in "Some Reflections on Political Nature: Conservative Theory Revisited," in *The Journal of Philosophy*, 72 (18) (1975), and I will borrow heavily from that article.

good society, then, is the society that fosters growth toward that maturity, providing whatever turns out to be needed for it and minimizing opportunities for incompatible courses of development. As for *natural humans*, they are quite secondary for the theory; we study them and their (and our!) animal origins only in order to discover more efficient ways to foster their growth to full humanity, by a better understanding of the tendencies hardwired into them. Untaught, unsocialized, the human is an interesting mass of potential, including potential for greed, violence, and murder most foul; rights and desires will be acquired only later, from the society. If the society is good, the rights and desires will be those conducive to growth to full humanity; if it is not, they will be otherwise. The task for every society, never-ending, is to channel the untaught potential of the natural human into the acquired role of the citizen, firmly thwarting greed and violence, encouraging cooperation.

As liberalism posits the satisfaction of individual desires or protection of rights as a good, so conservatism posits self-realization or the attainment of a fully functioning human life as a good: the assertion of value is at least in part independent of fact, not true by definition. (For example, we would want to deny that a fully functioning life for crabgrass, or a plague bacillus, is good.) As liberalism posits the individual as the starting point for association, since the individual's free choices will construct that association, so conservatism posits the association as the starting point for the individual, which is its most valued product. And finally, liberalism posits purposes or interests for individuals, but must deny them to associations; conservatism holds that associations above all have purposes, the highest association having the purpose of perfecting the individual, while individuals have only partial or derivative purposes.

The liberal orientation is, to our displeasure, considerably clearer and easier to understand than the conservative. We all know what it is to have desires, to feel pleasure and pain, and we have at least a working notion of a "right." But the conservative has to defend the proposition that there is a "good" condition of a human being, constituted by the fulfillment of the best of his potential, which is in some sense "natural" or "normal" for every person, even if no one perfectly embodies this condition. If this "good" condition is not the "typical" or "average" condition of the human – if we cannot discover it by surveys and measurements – how will we ever find out what it is? "Who's to say," (my sophomores' favorite question) "what 'the good' is?" Can it be more than subjective opinion? And then, the conservative has to defend the proposition that the society's chief, if not sole, duty, is to nurture that good human being to maturity.

The position is easier to defend if we ally it to the work we already do to raise children. There are values, generally agreed upon, governing the physical development of the human body. These intrinsic values (as opposed to instrumental values – great height for playing in the NBA, for instance) – health, and normal growth to maturity – are familiar and accepted. We have a working knowledge of what health is, we value it and seek to promote it, and we are acutely aware (especially in the case of our own children) of the importance of normal physical development. Health has valuable consequences, of course – freedom from pain, capacity to work, play, and enjoy life generally – but we do not have to value health and normal growth only for their consequences. They are perfectly understandable values all by themselves. From them, other values can be derived: healing is good, injury and prevention of healing is bad, growth to maturity is good, while blight, retardation, or failure of development

46

is bad. We know what normal health and maturity are, from centuries of empirical observations, even though we know nowhere near enough about the human body to specify exactly what characteristics *define* health or *define* maturity. But despite the fact that these values, these goals of action, are specifiable only as end states of some partially understood process, we have no difficulty whatsoever in affirming them and working with them.

And so it is with the health and growth of all human capacities. Normally we apply the same developmental reasoning to the acquisition of skills involving centers of the brain other than those governing the general maintenance of the body. Failure of a dog to run, a bird to fly, or a baby to walk and talk by a certain point of development (that point determined by observation of thousands of cases) is regarded as a failure regardless of the usefulness of these activities to society, and the cause of the failure is likely to be regarded as an unhealthy condition as well as a growth-blighting condition, despite other signs of the organism's contentment.

The development of the repertory of skills appropriate to each species is evaluated as is simple physical development, even though skills development is partially voluntary – the child has to *try* to learn to speak correctly, for instance. Our understanding of the desirable course for human development does not ordinarily change when we consider the emergence of higher capacities later in the process. We extend the assumption that "good" human capacities are the end-product of a "normal" development, up to and including the highest. Intellectual ability, for example, we treat like psychomotor ability, and we take the same attitude to moral development, holding persons with a history of brutalization less responsible for their actions than those raised in a "normal" environment. As with physical development, normal intellectual and moral development are presumed until evidence is introduced to the contrary, and the evidence must be of specific blight-inducing factors in the environment. No explanation is required for normal growth to maturity.

To find the moral characteristics of the "normal person," we may start by considering how we decide how people are "not normal" – retarded or disturbed, excluded from full participation in the society on account of some deficiency other than gross physical injury or conviction for crime. Some of them we call "sick" – explicitly recognizing, in its absence, a state of health desirable for them. Among them, of course, are those with subtle physical deficiency, but it is primarily their social functioning that is lacking. In most forms of mental or emotional "illness," the most conspicuous absence is the flexibility and openness to other human beings that we expect. Another apparent deficiency is intellectual functioning, or rationality – the ability to maintain fruitful perceptions of the world, logical patterns of thought, and organized patterns of behavior. Related to both is the deficiency in what we usually call *responsibility*: the disposition to consider others before acting, and to tailor courses of action to structures of duty and the expectations of other people. (It is usually this deficiency that made exclusion from society mandatory.) The "sick" or "incompetent" person is asocial, irrational, and irresponsible; from which it follows that essential qualities of full mental, emotional, and moral health are sociality, rationality, and responsibility. Fully embodying these qualities are the persons who are *autonomous*, able to choose their own directions, set their own standards, and obey rules that they have made their own – not invented from scratch out of some moral instinct, but learned, sorted, and refined from the directions, standards and rules they have absorbed from their communities. In this cluster of capacities and dispositions, I think we find the core of the conservative's "good person" – the standard for human development, the finest product of a good society. What, then, is the good society that will direct itself to nurturing that person?

Aristotle recognizes three levels of human association: the household, or family, the (tribal) village, and the *polis*, political association or state. Both liberals and conservatives recognize the importance of the family, as nurturing the youngsters to at least the appearance of adulthood, but both leave it behind as an essentially incomplete form of association. In the discussion of the next phase of human association, the liberal graduates a self-interested rational agent from the family, and has him contemplating the great undifferentiated mass of his fellow humans, asking himself "whether it is to my advantage to assume moral obligations to others?" It probably is not; but on the assumption that he decides it is, the liberal contracts him into a civil society whose only claim on the individual's duty is its consistency in providing the appointed benefits. (Curiously enough, this theoretical reduction of all associating to Individual and State lays the groundwork for all absolutism *and* all revolution.) The conservative, on the contrary, defends the proposition that the village, "tribal" association, precedes the political association, both psychologically (as a temporal phase of human development), and logically. The liberal's rational egoist is self-interested; but the concept of "self" is actually one of "self-as-opposed-to-other-selves," and the recognition of "self-interest" as opposed to "not-self-interest" depends on prior recognition of "common interest" or "group interest," as the notion of "one out of a group" depends on the notion of a "group." Further, the liberal's egoist is "reasonable": but "reasoning," thinking, is nothing other than the internalization of an essentially interpersonal communicative process. The "rational" person has internalized a public reasoning process, an extended many-person communication that has been improved and refined until it can be called "logical," probably by repeated correction by others in the public forum. The "egoist" has differentiated himself, his self, from all the others, a process which simply does not happen at the beginning levels of human growth and awareness.

For the liberal, the individual is the natural primitive, and association with the group has to be explained; for the conservative, the group is primitive, and the emergence of the individual is a group achievement. That natural group, beyond the family, is the village, physical or psychological, within which the individual's moral sense is nurtured and his moral maturity attained. The village sets the rules of dealing with others outside the family, monitors the individual's adherence to those rules, rewards and punishes, exhorts, rejoices and deplores, and generally provides the venue in which maturation, the achievement of what Aristotle would call "virtue," is possible. It should be noted, that at this level – between individual and state – there are a multitude of other associations that the conservative will defend: social clubs, service organizations, churches and other religious associations, guilds or labor unions, professional associations, literary clubs and all manner of private arrangements for education, exploration, and recreation. All of these help in socializing the individual, all of them reinforce the transparency of the society and the accountability of the individual to his or her companions.

Necessary Virtues

So the first error that defines the scandals, of Enron and all the others, is the mistaken belief that the individual, the I, having acquired enough material goods to buy insulation, privacy and anonymity, has no further obligation to the moral community that nurtured it. The individual, a little cluster of desires, knowledge, and rights, is expected to go ahead and seek his own greatest advantage. But this whole orientation ignores the role of human virtue, the achievement of human excellence.

Virtue includes all the separate virtues, conditions of excellence in the pursuit of the varied activities of human life. The virtues are not the same across society; the kinds of excellence cultivated by the athlete, for instance, are different from those cultivated by the scholar. Some virtues – honesty, willingness to work, generosity and a sense of humor – will serve well in all pursuits. But business has its own virtues, which militate strongly against the kind of abuse that we have seen in the recent scandals, and it may be worth taking a look at these.

The free market as Adam Smith intended it to work had serious safeguards, to prevent the abuses that we have seen in recent years. While external regulation was strongly condemned, and government urged to stay out of the workings of the market, Smith assumed that there would continue to be the kind of regulation that human society had always known, the reaction of the neighbors. Business would not succeed unless the participants had certain qualities: honesty, integrity, industry, and conscientious attention to all affected by the market. For business was practiced in a village, the same context that humans knew from long before capitalism, possibly long before agriculture. The businessman dealt with people he had known since childhood, and every dealing was known to many people. The businessman who cheated a customer would be found out immediately. Accounting practices were much simpler; the businessman who cheated his partner (or his investors) would be found out in not much longer. In the face to face situation of the village, where repeat business was essential to solvency, such virtuous practices were merely the condition for staying in business; honesty was, as above, indeed the best policy and virtue was prudence. Smith thought that such virtues inhered in individuals, and would be a permanent part of the character even in contexts outside the village. Conservatives thought that they were possible only as long as the village continued, and fought to retain the village in its pure form, even arguing for the necessity of useless rituals and traditional hierarchy and privilege which were clearly unjust. They were both partly wrong.

The executives currently or recently on trial for their offenses against the law clearly failed in their duties of stewardship toward the enterprises with which they were entrusted. But their failure had been made easier for them, if not inevitable, by changes in the context of business. They had helped to contribute to the changes, but they were by no means alone.

The Collapse of Every Restriction

Two major losses precede the scandals. The first, obvious, loss, is the dismantling of the regulatory framework that had been set up to control businesses that had flown out of control the last time this happened, in the late 1920s. In those high-flying years also, corporate officers of great personal wealth and power systematically cheated the public, customers and investors and citizens alike, for personal gain. In the period of national repentance that followed, during the 1930s, strong procedures were put in place to control how banks, corporations, and the securities markets operated. Utilities, energy provision, were carefully regulated; corporate financial transparency was assured by the appointment of independent auditors from newly formed accounting firms; anti-trust provisions were established to reduce the harmful concentrations of power that had done so much damage to the economy in the previous decade; strict reporting provisions were laid down. All of these got in the way of certain kinds of lucrative arrangements, but that, of course was the point: the public had had its fill of lucrative arrangements that enriched a few businessmen and hurt everyone else.

Half a century later (when all the victims had died), during the 1980s, a concerted attack against regulations, all regulations, was mounted by certain representatives of American business, strongly supported by the pro-business administration of President Ronald Reagan. Reagan believed deeply in the perfection of the Free Market, in the purest Adam Smith interpretation as he understood it: keep government out of the market, let each product and service find its own price, and competition will drive down the costs and benefit the consumer. Any government interference, he honestly believed, only makes the market less efficient and hurts everyone, producer and consumer alike. As the elder Bush succeeded Reagan, legislation repealing regulatory regimes dating back to the 1930s began to emerge.

This is no place to go into the details of "regulation," but some background is required. Since the second third of the twentieth century at least, there was a broad consensus that goods and services which were both *necessary* and *natural monopolies* should be "utilities," working under the control of government agencies, which would regulate their capacity and their prices, supply and demand. Goods which were necessary (like food) but in which it was impossible for one producer to establish a monopoly or anything like a monopoly, could be left to the free market; goods which were natural monopolies or oligopolies, but the purchase of which could be deferred and negotiated, like coal and steel, could also be left (uneasily) to the free market. But where the entire water supply for a region is owned by one company, it would be foolhardy to leave the pricing to that company; it could charge any amount it wanted, and people would have to pay. Like water, energy – gas and electricity supplied to homes and businesses – had always been regulated, when it was not supplied by government itself. Regulation had always bothered investors in energy companies, for although they appreciated the reliability of the income, they were sure that income could be a lot higher, at least that is what they were told by the executives, if only regulation could be removed. With administrations friendly to business in place, they felt they had a very good chance to get burdensome regulation removed. Kenneth Lay of Enron led the charge, making enormous contributions to the campaigns of Democrats and Republicans alike, but especially to the presidential campaign of fellow Texan George W. Bush. The point was to force the deregulation of the electric utilities in California, where Enron was aiming to dominate the market. They succeeded in obtaining the deregulation, and promptly did what everyone said a deregulated utility would do: they shut down perfectly good capacity in order to drive up the price, then forced the State of California to sign long-term contracts for energy at the higher price, then turned the power back on and walked away with tens of millions of California taxpayer dollars. When last heard from, the federal courts were enforcing those contracts, even as the emails detailing the plots were coming to light. There has been, in this administration to this point, no backlash in favor of reinstating an adequate regulatory scheme. In California, at least, the loss of the regulatory regime is etched on the citizens' consciousness.

The second, less obvious loss, is the collapse of the country club (or the club generally; it doesn't have to be in the country). The clubs are still there, but one of their functions has changed, the function of serving as a moral village for the wealthy. The grand wealth-condensing engines of the 1980s, for instance, the hostile takeovers, were outside the pale of acceptable participation for most of the twentieth century. Prior to the 1980s, those who would be "raiders" were ostracized, corporate lawyers would not participate in such "deals," it was understood that venerable corporations, with their historic missions and their large numbers of jobs, were to be preserved. Also out of bounds were corporate bankruptcies (except in the most extreme circumstances), massive layoffs (except in financial exigency, when *all* salaries were reduced, starting with the highest), and the granting of outsized executive bonuses and other compensation. None of these measures were illegal, at least not in and of themselves. But to engineer layoffs in order to boost profits (and bonuses) was to fail, very seriously, in the executive's duty of stewardship of the business, and to attack the corporations was to assault your co-stewards – the other members of the club, yours or one very like it in another town. The country club enforced socially the provisions that could not be enforced legally – provisions of moderation, compassion, restraint, decency, and proportion. Greed was simply bad taste. The business press of the time followed the country club in praising the good citizens and ostracizing the bad ones.

No one ever mounted an attack against the country club; it collapsed under the pressures of money and globalization. While the club worked, it worked because all the money in American business was, one way or another, in the club. In the 1980s a series of developments – deregulation of certain kinds of mergers, the sudden market in junk bonds, the automation of stock trading – led to large amounts of money suddenly available for corporate takeovers in a situation where the corporations found themselves completely out of control of their stock, their companies suddenly in play in a very fast-moving action that they had no way of stopping. Suddenly money was flowing through the markets at a speed, and in an amount, unheard of; in the investment banks and brokerages, the young traders who could find a part in this action ignored the older partners and the customary barriers. The new culture said, if it brings in money, it's all right; the technology was available to transfer huge amounts of money in seconds; the young men on the trading desks heard the message loud and clear, and simply shoved the older ones aside. At first, they ignored the country club; in the end, the country club was only too glad to welcome them and their money in through its doors.

Globalization dealt the final blow to the country club, at least as a moral school for young businessmen. The power of the country club came not only from its monopoly on all the money in town, but from its monopoly of all the people who dealt in money. Even in the early 1950s companies did business abroad, but one could still count on a Power Elite in every town, constituted of all the local businessmen who controlled any significant wealth, and whose approval was necessary for anyone new doing any significant business in town. As the Internet became the property of all, as first faxes, then email, connected businesses globally, the financial power of any locality became diffused, then disappeared. There were still clubs – there will always be clubs – but their power to control the financial activities of their members and those who aspired to membership has gone.

The business press, as a final footnote here, has followed the money, taking on something of the customs of the Hollywood press that follows the movie stars. In *Forbes*, October 2003, Dan Ackman oozed contempt for the pitiful Dennis Kozlowski of Tyco, based on the video of his infamous birthday bash for his wife on the island of Sardinia; he dismissed Kozlowski as "an unamusing toastmaster and a God-awful dancer. Instead of looking like *Joe Millionaire*, Kozlowski seemed to be auditioning for *Queer Eye for the Straight Guy*."[4] How have the mighty fallen, from the heights of praise to the level of homosexual wannabe! Two years before, *Business Week* had Kozlowski as one of "the top 25 managers – managers to watch," and oozed adoration instead. "This Midas touch in deal after deal has transformed Tyco from an obscure manufacturer into a powerhouse worth 50 times more than when Kozlowski took charge eight years ago. It's an achievement that has led some to compare Kozlowski with General Electric Co.'s Jack Welch. But unlike Welch, Kozlowski shows no signs of slowing down anytime soon."[5] Meditate, shall we, on the fawning tone of *Business Week* in that article, that came out just when Kozlowski's extravagances and abuses were getting into high gear. Can that article have helped the situation? Can we – could we ever – expect more vigilance, more sense of right and wrong, of the business press?

[4] Forbes.com, Top Of The News, Dan Ackman, "L. Dennis Kozlowski Is Not Fabulous," October 29, 2003; www.forbes.com/ 2003/10/29/cx_da_1029topnews.
[5] Dennis Kozlowski, Tyco International; www.businessweek.com/ 2001/01_02/b3714009.htm

The Transformation of the Landscape

Out of these losses – the collapse of the regulatory system, the prostitution of the country club, the abdication of the business press – rose the precursors of the grand theft corporate to which we have been the witnesses. A look at the quiet, almost stealthy, moves of a new economy will help us put the scandals in a larger business context. Two major changes in the moral psychology of the business world had to occur before an Enron could happen. (A note to the literal-minded: in what follows we will contrast the practices of the corporate giants of the 1950s with the very different practices of business in 2005. Please believe that we know that such generalizations cannot possibly be literally true. But we are taking into account not only what businesses actually do, but also the way they portray themselves, on ground that such portrayals serve as the guides and role models for the next practices. If they help us to focus on the vice that has left our business system in moral tatters, and help us get a handle on how we might do something to restore it to credibility, then they have been useful enough for our purposes.)

First was the final abandonment of the notion of the responsibility of the wealthy for the fate of the nation, and the return to an outsized sense of material entitlement. It had been a matter of some amusement, and disgust, to their educated contemporaries, that the Captains of Industry of the nineteenth century, reading all the literature they could get their hands on detailing the glories of the courts of the Pharaohs, had set out to recreate for themselves the storied luxuries of the East. Nothing was too good for them. In their time, the rich paraded their riches before the commoners, to enhance their sense of grandeur and to awe the poor into keeping their place. They were roundly condemned, not just by the brand-new Marxists, but by the tradesman middle class (Ben Franklin's people) and above all by the healthy remainder of the tightly disciplined Protestant Christian society that had founded most of the towns then in the United States. Vainglory was evil; purchasing objects just for display was wrong; all material indulgence beyond what was necessary for a healthy life was vanity, waste, and most assuredly annoying to the Almighty as a violation of the rules of prudence and frugality that had governed American life from the beginning (at least on the surface). Surfaces are important. Despite their enormous power, these capitalists and their trusts had to bow before President Theodore Roosevelt's trustbusting crusades, backed by the populists of the newly organized countryside and the budding labor unions. The material extravagance returned in the 1920s, very briefly, then got blown out of the water by the collapse of the NYSE and the Great Depression. Not everyone became poor, but the "malefactors of great wealth," as one government prosecutor called them, became very humble, at least when prosecutors were around.

The Second World War proved a great equalizer: for the first time, rich and poor served together, for a long time, in deadly combat, and at the end wanted nothing more than to return to a stable life. The war taxes had wiped out many of the great estates. The GI Bill sent the working class to college. The suburbs blurred the boundaries among the hardworking farms, the country seats of the landed gentry, and the immigrant cities. Towns lavished money on their public schools. The visible face of America was egalitarian, hardworking, upwardly mobile, reliable, patriotic, child-friendly, and not given to extravagance. The 1960s made dogma out of the *de facto* equality achieved by the war. But after the turmoil of the 1970s, the message of the election in 1980 was that responsibility, hard work and stewardship, the bywords of the generation that went to war, need not occupy quite so much of the national life: Let us enjoy ourselves. Small fortunes had been quietly amassed during the 1970s (especially by those on the right side of the oil embargo), and money was itching to be spent. Slowly the ante of living rich, living very rich, went up, and some of its products now are part of our daily life – the private houses called the McMansions, for instance, so called because no matter how large and studded with expensive features they are, they somehow all look alike; the modification of those mansions to include electronic features that no one would have thought to put in a private home before, like home theaters; the multiplication of the houses owned by one family; the emerging standard of the three-car garage; the bewildering number of luxury "performance" cars to put in those garages, including cars that only exist to be extravagant (one thinks of General Motors's "Hummers," whose major reason for being, in the absence of hostile mortar fire on the LA Freeway, seems to be the consumption of outsized amounts of expensive fuel). From these the whole "consumer" culture, noticeable from the 1960s onward, developed, spread to the Mall, and took over much too much of our lives. There was one glaring omission in the Return to Luxury: the previous rich, the rich of the nineteenth and early twentieth centuries, had been the major support of the arts, subsidizing the opera, purchasing collections for the art museums, and patronizing the symphony orchestras. They also endowed their colleges with new Science Buildings and libraries, sponsored theaters, and supported the Red Cross. The new rich do none of that. They watch TV, on huge flat screens in their home theaters.[6] From an aristocracy of inherited

---

[6] There are exceptions. Consider Bill and Melinda Gates's work in supporting efforts to improve the health of children worldwide.

gentility, that took seriously its obligations to maintain the culture they had inherited, we have moved instead to an aristocracy of extravagant entitlement.

The move from responsibility to entitlement shatters all the bonds that restrained consumption. It is not out of envy that the press never mentions Dennis Kozlowski without mentioning that ice statue at the $600 million party he threw for his wife, and the $6,000 shower curtain. Never mind that no one was hurt by that shower curtain, and that he had every right to buy any shower curtain he wanted on the open market, etc. etc. All else being equal, that is just obscenely too much to pay for a shower curtain. Everyone knows that. Possibly there are extenuating circumstances – it's only money, and we're willing to negotiate – but none have been suggested. Like our Puritan ancestors, we know when the permissible limits of material consumption have been reached and breached.

Second, business practices started to change in the 1980s. One of the major topics in the Business Ethics literature of the day, we may recall, was the "hostile takeover." Without getting into the technicalities, the hostile takeover was the purchase of a company against the will of its board of directors, thus to be distinguished from a normal "merger" of two companies who think they can make it better together than alone, or a simple "acquisition" of one company by another with full cooperation of the board of directors. The difference between the hostile and the friendly operations is only that in a friendly takeover, the board of the company being acquired might be expected to protect the interests of all the stakeholders – shareholders, employees, suppliers, customers, and the local community – whereas in the hostile kind, no such opportunity exists.

A publicly held corporation is, after all, nothing but a piece of paper. The living company, the grand corporate citizen of the 1950s, rich with tradition, inspired by a narrative of success, nurturing its customers, employees and shareholders alike as family, sponsoring Little League teams and arts exhibitions, protecting its workers with a well-funded pension fund and health care benefits, freely lending employees and expertise to solve public problems, a thriving and vibrant community centered in the towns it has helped to build – all that is an accident, legally non-existent, embodying no rights, only a fiction. The reality is that any party (hereinafter "raider," and occasionally, "shark") with enough money can purchase a controlling block of shares, supposing the shareholders are willing to sell them, and at that point that party owns the company. He can abolish the Little League teams and the charities overnight (and probably will), he can lay off two-thirds of the workers, ending their health insurance and other benefits, he can close their plants, selling off the buildings and machines, he can raid the pension funds for the cash to pay off the loans he took out to buy the company to begin with and walk off with the rest (he'll probably do that, too), and with that extra cash he can put a down payment on the next company he intends to strip. How can this be legal, or right? But, on the argument that a new owner might be able to get the shareholders a higher return on their investment by using the company's assets more efficiently, it is held to be right, and it is certainly legal. Why did it happen? Three new business developments in the 1980s supported the surge of hostile takeovers.

First, there was a significant change in the ownership of the stock in publicly held companies. The grand corporate citizen (see above) used to be owned by millions of individual shareholders, including some wealthy individuals with large blocks of shares. Those owners, especially the small group of large shareholders (who may have been among the company's founders), bought the stock because they believed in the company's future, willed it to their favorite children, followed the company's fortunes eagerly (including the Little League team), and defended it fiercely in public controversy. Not all of them, of course, but many of the shareholders were proud and loyal owners, identifying themselves as part of the company, and would never have dreamed of selling their shares to someone who promised them a quick profit, a higher price for their shares than the market would have predicted, in return for the right to destroy the company. At the least, they expected more in future returns on that investment than they would be able to get with any other use of the cash they would receive for the stock. But times had changed. Starting in the 1960s, ownership of publicly held companies was absorbed by funds – mutual funds of all description, and including the huge pension funds and university endowment funds which had previously invested only in ultra-safe bonds. When these funds changed their strategy from creditorship to ownership, in many cases they displaced the wealthy individuals who had been the influential owners, and effectively took over control of those companies. These funds were incapable of feeling pride and loyalty to anything whatever. Given their structure, feelings hardly mattered; the managers of the funds were in effect trustees for the contributors (those who would, for instance, be receiving the pensions when they retired), and had no charge but to increase the value of the fund. They had very little interest in the hopeful future of any of the companies whose shares they held. All that mattered was the value of the stock, and they monitored the stock market moment to moment to track that value. Offered a price for their shares that was higher than could be expected in the market, they had no choice but to accept, and they could turn the cash around immediately into a more profitable investment. The most profitable investment, of course, was the next takeover target, since the raider would always offer a higher price than the market had sustained, and the managers could expect a very rapid increase in the value of the fund's portfolio. The takeover phenomenon fed on itself. The net result of these developments is that individual shareholders became insignificant in the market; not only had they lost the effective right to veto takeovers of companies they knew they held, but their major holdings, through their pension funds, were completely inaccessible and invisible to them. The people whose money it was, had lost all control over how it might be spent in the stock market, and their money had taken on a direction of its own – always to further growth. Money, barren iron in Aristotle's term, had learned to breed.

The second significant change in the business world was the legitimization of that hostile takeover, its acceptance into the day to day operations of business, and by extension the legitimization of the most ruthless of the Mergers and Acquisitions activities of the raiders and the investment bankers that funded them. A particularly clever bond broker, Michael Milken of Drexel Burnham Lambert, discovered a huge market in low-cost high-yield "junk" bonds, which could be used to provide the awesome amounts of cash needed for the takeovers; his accomplishments were celebrated yearly in a "Predator's Ball," where budding young raiders were helped to put together takeover bids with the near-unlimited loans available. Milken was skating very close to the line between what was legal and what was not, as he knew and of which he boasted. The scheming and profit-taking could not work without illegal insider trading, for which Milken was indicted in 1989. (Eventually he pled guilty to securities fraud, was sentenced to prison for 10 years, got out in two years because he was ill with prostate cancer; as of 2003 he was still quite alive, running a philanthropy from the Milken Family

Foundation, established with the millions he had made trading junk bonds, to battle cancer.)

Here, in the depredations of the junk bond masters and the gleeful raiders, long past any claim that they can "marshal the company's assets more efficiently for the benefit of the shareholders," we feel most keenly the loss of the country club. The prime movers in this orgy of greed, brokers and bankers, had never had the responsibility or experience of running a large company, or indeed any enterprise at all. In their eyes, "the company" finally reduced to no more than an opportunity to extract large amounts of cash from legal ownership of a legal fiction, and they proceeded with no regard to the people, from middle management on down, who got hurt. (Often top management could be paid to abandon resistance to the takeover, and sometimes that pay went into the millions.) In the politer society of the 1950s, when all radical changes in arrangements were frowned on, and if harmful, could be stopped by peer pressure, none of this would be possible. Whatever of the "village" the club had been able to create was gone. Peers could no longer control peers; elders could no longer control their juniors. The senior executives, in bank, brokerage, or target company, were simply shoved aside as the cash rolled in from the Mergers and Acquisitions Department.

The third significant change was a radical alteration in the social contract between corporations and their stakeholders. As late as the mid-1970s, the new "business ethics" (or "social issues management") community had been talking about a "new social contract," one in which business took more responsibility for the welfare of their workers and of the communities in which their plants were located. James Beré, CEO of Borg Warner, had characterized the corporation as a "guest" in the community, with strong obligations to tailor its actions to the common good. All that disappeared completely in the new Greed society, as a new Social Contract did indeed emerge – and not one the ethicists would have wanted. Again, it all started in the early 1980s, with the closing of "unprofitable" plants in several industries, especially the old industries on which the nation had been built – coal, iron, and steel. Often the plants were not losing money, but their profitability was lower than could be found in other industries, and their owners felt that they could not compete successfully for capital. Capital was often what was needed; as Japan was tearing down its 1950s steel plants to put up newer and more efficient ones, our 1930s steel plants continued to operate, held together by baling wire. The managers of the companies solemnly cited their obligations to the shareholders, laid off the workers and closed the plants – notoriously, often after extracting years of subsidies and tax concessions from the communities in which they had operated, not to mention wage concessions from the workers, on the promise that the plants would be kept working. Sometimes municipalities sued, unsuccessfully, to recover the amount that the taxpayers had invested to keep the plant open.

While we are still on the subject of the 1980s layoffs at the old manufacturing plants, this might be the place to ask – why is there no recourse in these incidents? To be sure, no one ever signed a contract saying, workers will be employed for life, and this company will always have a plant in this town, pouring money into the local economy. But consider: if a woman hangs out with a man, servicing his needs, maybe having his children, without any contract of marriage, in five years she's a common law wife. If he takes off after a younger lady after 20 years, she can get "palimony," as it is called, money from the departing man, which will at least help her get back on her feet. Note that a common defense mounted by the man, is that "I supported her all those years, paid for her food, put a roof over her head, took her to the movies on Saturday. Isn't that enough?" That's rather like the company insisting that its obligations to its workers were completely fulfilled by payment of wages and contractual benefits during his time of employment. But also note that the man often loses these cases: time itself counts, and all that time, especially since the woman is now older and less marriageable, builds up an entitlement. *In the Common Law, using up a person's life is something that should be paid for.* Now, why doesn't the worker, who at 53 is unemployable but not yet eligible for Social Security, have the same right?

The structure of executive compensation also changed in the 1980s. In an effort to make managers more "accountable" to the desire of the shareholders for more money, compensation for the higher officers of the company was often paid in stock options (since that would give the managers an incentive to make the value of the stock go up), and the CEO especially was awarded a yearly bonus, often much more than his salary, on the basis of the rise or fall of the value of the stock. (Just to keep ourselves in line with the 1950s corporation we left behind, note that the quality of the firm's product, the prudence of the investments in future capacity, the careful balancing of short and long term, does not figure in this equation. The shareholder – most likely an impersonal fund, see above – is not presumed to be the least interested in long-term return on investment. The shareholder wants value now.)

Let us take brief note on how the structure of incentives in business has changed. In the 1950s, the business ideal had the CEO paid well, certainly – as much as $50,000 to $75,000 (quite generous when corrected for inflation) – but rewarded much more significantly with the appreciation of the communities in which the company operated as a major taxpayer and a major employer. Not the least of the intangible rewards was the appreciation of his knowledgeable peers, as expressed in the country club. There were ways to make more money, even then, but often as not a more active regulatory system would suggest the unwisdom of risky schemes, and the disapproval of the peers – who were, after all, likely to be among the first ones hurt in a hostile takeover – might deter risky behavior before it started. A major incentive was simple pride in the company: the knowledge that it was in good financial shape, doing good work and supporting its people. When markets changed (and they did, even then) layoffs might become inevitable and factories forced to close, but these were occasions of deep sorrow and shame for the CEO, who felt himself responsible for the failure; in most instances, the salaries of the top managers were reduced in proportion to the damage done to the workers.

The new incentives for the CEO are radically different. Most unfortunately, the intangibles seem to be gone, and the motivation restricted to money, leaving competitive type-A men (and increasingly, women) to compete only for money. As compensation committees will candidly concede, one reason that CEOs are paid so much now is that, like top-ranked professional basketball players, they regard it as humiliating to be paid less than a certain percentage of the compensation of their peers, who function now as a spur to greater and greater greed rather than as a weight for moderation. Pride in one's compensation has replaced pride in the company. The only way to ensure more compensation is to keep increasing the value of the shares. Since that value is computed in part as a ratio of return on investment, income over costs, the easiest way to increase it is to cut costs, and the easiest way to do that is to lay off as many employees as possible, cutting payments and benefits to the rest. When the company was the object of pride, layoffs disgraced a CEO, and he was expected to share the loss; now, the layoff is strongly rewarded by the shareholders, and the CEO gets to share in the profits. When costs have been reduced as far as possible, with no new income in sight, bonuses will drop sharply unless the CEO can arrange to have the company at least *appear* to be doing well, a task at which CEOs are increasingly skilled. (See HealthSouth, above.) As we found out only recently, after significant scholarship on the subject, rewarding CEOs with stock options and adjusting bonuses to the value of the stock create an excellent incentive to cook the books in order to keep the value of the shares advancing.

The Pension Betrayal

The most recent transformation is the most devastating. Throughout the life of the corporation, from the Second World War to the present day, workers have accepted lower wage increases in return for health care plans and rock-solid contractual guarantees of retirement benefits. Part of the American Dream, beyond the well-paid job and college for the children, was the comfortable retirement, "golden years" when there would be no financial worries because of the well-funded pension plan held by the company. The key to the American Retirement was the "defined benefits" plan: each worker, depending on what he or she made during employment with the company, upon retirement, will receive a certain amount per month for the rest of his or her life. The company's promise was based, of course, on the assumption that while some workers would live to a comfortable 95, many others would die in their late sixties and seventies, and there would be enough to pay for everyone.

Only recently have we seen that the promise was not to be kept. The problem began, here as elsewhere, with the hostile takeovers. Early in the 1980s, Congress had authorized the use of "excess" money in "overfunded" pension funds to serve the general purposes of the company; the raider simply pronounced the pension fund "overfunded," used part of it to purchase annuities that would substitute for the pension when the time came for workers to retire, and pocketed the rest. Of course, if the annuities did not have a solid foundation, the workers could lose everything – and often did. (When Pacific Lumber's insurance program, for instance, went bankrupt, the workers lost the annuities that the raider, Charles Hurwitz, had purchased to replace the rich pension fund he had drained. Turned out the insurance company's guarantees were based, like Hurwitz's loan, on Michael Milken's junk bonds.) Through the 1980s, an estimated $21 billion that had been set aside for workers' pensions was appropriated by the raiders. Eventually, in 1990, Congress passed legislation taxing money grabbed from pension funds, and corporate raids slowed way down – the big pot of gold was no longer there for the grab.[7]

By the twenty-first century, corporate defaults and bankruptcies were ending pension plans all over the corporate map. Companies had cavalierly miscalculated their pension liabilities (by, for instance, assuming that a much higher interest rate than prevailed would raise the value of the plan) and took "funding holidays" when times were bad; after all, most pension obligations are in the future, and are therefore the last to be taken care of. Law forbade most of the practices whereby companies dodged their obligations, but companies (especially airlines) lobbied for changes in the laws, and got them, so that they could

[7]   Donald L. Barlett and James B. Steele, "The Broken Promise," *Time*, October 31, 2005, pp. 32ff.

base their promises on more and more optimistic assumptions about the future of the economy. State and local budgets are in the same bad shape as the companies, since they also promise rich benefits, and it's going to be harder for them to shrug off the obligations. As a matter of fact, it's going to be impossible: by law, those obligations have to be paid, so municipalities will have to raise taxes or float bonds to pay them.

To protect the workers, Congress set up the Pension Benefit Guaranty Corporation (PBGC), funded by a tax on all corporations that offer pension benefits, to guarantee pensions for workers in corporations that had abandoned the promised plans. It was in trouble from the start, as we probably should have known. Since companies are not required to offer pensions, many younger companies (like Dell) do not, and the older companies have to compete with them *and* take responsibility for paying into the PBGC. This is not a stable arrangement.

The PBGC was set up to provide a floor for benefits – to make sure that pension funds were well funded, and to take up the protection of the workers if the companies could no longer do so. At one point it tried, as part of efforts to keep plans well funded, publishing a list of the underfunded ones; that idea, anathema to corporations, was shot down by Congress. The PBGC is supposed to supply a safety net, based on revenues from industry, to pay out pensions. Right now pension obligations are either $450 billion or $600 billion in arrears, depending on how you count, and the debt is growing. It is difficult to plan for future obligations; when companies cave in and give their debts to the PBGC, the debts are always understated, due to inadequate reporting requirements – also passed by Congress.

The pattern is established: soon, all companies with defined benefit plans will give them over to the PBGC, which is already

$23 billion down, headed for $30 billion. Recall, the way the PBGC works, it gets no taxpayer dollars. It is funded by assessments from companies that still have defined-benefits plans, which means its very existence gives them a powerful incentive to drop theirs. The overwhelming temptation for most companies is to move from defined benefit plans to defined contribution plans, the ubiquitous 401(k), where the worker gets out of the plan essentially only what he puts in, sometimes matched by the company. But 401(k)s are not pensions. All they are is a license to defer taxes on money the worker himself puts into the fund. In the early 1980s, when 401(k)s started, the stock market started on a wild upswing, so the future looked very good and no one worried about pensions very much. But there are two problems with these accounts: First, the money contributed by the worker is really not in the bank, it's in the company, and if the company goes broke, all those contributions are lost. Workers depend on 401(k)s, and went along with them when they were introduced because "that's your money, it's owed to you, you can't lose it." Except you can. Second, in any case, it's not a lot of money. Half of all 401(k)s are worth less than $18,000, and a quarter, less than $5,000. That won't go very far. In the future, Americans will have two choices: they can arrange to be very rich, in which case companies will shower pensions on them worth tens of millions of dollars, or they can be poor, in which case they can collect cans for a living or just go on working.

The Hood Robin Syndrome

A pattern begins to emerge from the confusion. Not everyone emerges from this general collapse poor. As above, every time workers are laid off or forced into wage concessions, the CEO's pay goes up. Pensions also turn into gold: when the pension plan of a company is shut down and the obligation turned over to the federal government, the company becomes much more valuable (more costs are cut) and the shareholders and the managers paid in stock options stand to profit magnificently.[8] Meanwhile, the consultants, the money managers, the bankers who have participated in managing the plan, all have to be paid, and paid generously, for their work.[9] These findings, little intriguing bits in the midst of the scandals, are of a piece with the "tax reform" instituted by the Republican administration that came to power in the year 2000; taxes were substantially lowered for the richest Americans, while programs for the poorest Americans were cut or (what amounts to the same thing) made much more difficult to access. Essentially, we are watching in our own time a dramatic redistribution of the wealth of America. It started in the Reagan administration, when the horrifying graphs made the front pages of major newspapers and feature articles in leading newsmagazines: for the first time since the War, the rich were getting richer and the poor were getting poorer, and the divergent lines on the graph had suggestive hooks on the end – the very rich were getting much richer, faster, and the very poor were getting much poorer, faster. Serious articles wondered if we would lose our middle class. From the start of the twenty-first century, the

[8]   Mary Williams Walsh, "Whoops! There Goes Another Pension Plan: Retiree Benefits Turn Into Gold For Wall Street," *The New York Times*, September 18, 2005, section 3 (BU), pp. 1, 9.
[9]   Mary Williams Walsh, "How Wall Street Wrecked United's Pension: Money Managers Were Paid in Full, But (Oops!) Retirees Won't Be," *The New York Times*, July 31, 2005, section 3, pp. 1, 8.

process has accelerated, and with all the developments charted in the last sections of this paper, it continues to accelerate. While Pope John Paul II asked us to incorporate into our policies a "preferential option for the poor," we have managed to enact, in a thousand ways, a "preferential option for the rich." Why is this?

We are reminded of Robin Hood, who in the face of radical injustice in his own time and his own land, undertook to rob the rich to give to the poor. In our land in our own time, we have embarked on a much more serious mission, to take from the poor and from the workers in order to give to the rich and to Wall Street. In so doing, we have created a new entitlement, as well established by now as Social Security (last bastion of the workers, itself under threat in the last year). The new entitlement is to become richer, by any means that suggest themselves, holding in contempt any law (dismissed as bureaucratic interference) or any counsel of moderation (dismissed as naive) or any cry of injustice (dismissed as "class warfare.") In all cases, the one who enriches himself is already rich, the loser in the contest is one who is already poor, marginalized, and unlucky. We have invented a new form of wealth transfer, that we may call the "Hood Robin" syndrome, Robin Hood in reverse, which legitimizes in advance any appropriation by the overprivileged of the undefended funds of the less advantaged.

Permission to Steal

Where does the permission to steal come from, then? The fountains of evil are deep within ourselves, not through demonic influence (although that interpretation is always tempting) but through ingrained, inherited, tendencies to engage in violent, lustful and greedy behavior, left over from the uncertain times in which the human race developed and when such tendencies aided survival – not all the time, never all the time, but just at those times when structures collapsed and survival was most threatened. We are the children of the survivors. They are not evil in themselves. But they have to be kept firmly under control if we are to live in a civilized society. The good news (that has sustained us through of our civilized existence) is that they can, indeed, be kept under control and turned to good purposes, and that the means to do this is very simple. We do not need terribly strict laws, harsh criminal sentences, guns, or cops; as a matter of fact, external controls of that sort may be counterproductive. We cannot do it through moral preaching, Character Formation classes, or exhortations to self-control; individual "strength of will" melts in front of temptation. But we do need witnesses. In the public light of day, completely visible, with everyone watching, we will not do what we know to be wrong. In the village, where everyone is watching all the time, and where we are expected to be able to give an account of ourselves and our actions to our neighbors, we will not do what we and the villagers hold to be wrong. The important point about those witnesses is that they need not be physically present. St. Paul talks about the "cloud of witnesses," saints and martyrs, that attended the young Christian Church through its early tumultuous years. At a time when new Christians had to leave their villages, or defy their traditions, Paul gave them a new village, of witnesses far and near, living and dead, to whom they would be accountable.

Witnesses determine conduct, whether we are talking about the witnesses to our own conduct, or to the conduct of those holding positions of responsibility in the largest businesses. The point of invisibility is that there are no witnesses, physically present or otherwise. The catastrophic collapse of morality in business came because of the retreat of the witnesses – the shredding of the social fabric and the release of the individual to act on his own convictions and conscience. Convictions and conscience are not enough, apparently. What shall we do? In the absence of inherited villages, can we make our own? It will not be easy, for anonymity is clearly in the interests of some very powerful people, and they will fight to keep it. Yet this seems to be where our trail leads. Can we do it?

3

Humility and Hope

Turning the Elephant

Hundreds of millions, billions, of America's money, our money, has been looted by thieves in the highest places in the land. If these were ordinary bank robbers, holding guns in people's faces, we would have mobilized the Marines to catch them before a fraction of what has been stolen, had been stolen, and we'd have put them in the maximum security wings of the most severe prisons we own. What do we have to do to restore law and order in the polite realms of very great wealth? I see seven tasks before us, to bring ourselves back to a point where we can trust our nation's wealthiest not to rob us.

Our *first* task is to gather the conviction to start on the path to an integrated and healthy society. It will not be the same trail that led to this dead end; no simple reversal of course is possible. It won't do just to scan the horizon for a pendulum backswing, while remaining silent; it is necessary to make the change happen. The first job is to recognize that it has to be done, and to gather the desire to do it. Why, after all, have we not experienced the outrage that would have overtaken the bank robbers? The difficulty lies in the ambivalence we still feel – incorporating both moments of the business press, adoration and contempt – for the disgraced businessmen. *For we are not an envious nation, and there is much in us which admires the thieves.* Take another look in that mirror. When we hear about the white collar thief who made off with $20 million while the employees lost their pensions, part of us says: he got that because he's smart; I wish I could get that too; maybe if I'm nice to him he'll share it with me; at least let's not change the system so I could never get that rich.

Why do we do this? Remember: there are dispositions, not all of them admirable, for which we are hardwired. When the old stabilities seem to be falling apart, in the shifting alliances of economic life, our dispositions revert to the foraging life, and nothing is more attractive than power. Survival, we recall, went not only to those who could seize and use power, but to those who quickly learned to ally themselves with power. We are their children.

Picking Up the Pieces

Our *second* task is to rebuild our public life. The ideology of "freedom" has left in its wake a conviction that the contemplation and use of public agency is somehow wrong – that "government" is always the enemy. (They tell the tale of Ronald Reagan, that he spent eight years as the most powerful government leader in the world, and at the end of it he *still* thought that government was the problem.) In reality, government is not Other, government is us, acting collectively instead of individually. The freedom of collective action has been assaulted and crippled in the present ideological atmosphere; a new timidity regarding the use of our collective power has turned us into the "pitiful, helpless giant" at home and abroad that we have long feared.

We have the right to start at the national level, to make sure that every representative elected to Congress carries to his desk the fear of God, and the fear of us. If face to face with the lobbyists for the mining industry, and with arm-twisting party leaders who serve the lobbyists, the representative continually faced the "cloud of witnesses" of the neighbors back home, who trust him, who expect him to work for their interests, and who will hold him to account if he does not, we may expect to have much better representation. The problem with this approach is that it only works if (as Thomas Jefferson supposed it always would) the representative is elected by a real village. If he (or she) is simply the chosen of the party machine, it is the party machine that will haunt his conversations, and that won't do us any good at all. If he is simply the agent of huge campaign contributions from the agricultural or mining interests, or the gun lobby, he will do us more harm than good. We have to make sure that his representation is authentic – that he really represents something, and that we are part of it.

But how can we do that? The villages themselves are in trouble, and we might do better to start at the local level, the level of the villages. If we think of public action, town action, as what we and our neighbors decide to do together (because it's something we cannot do alone) possibly the bugbear of "government," seen as government regulation, will lose its terrors, and possibly the fantasy of government as some distant cornucopia, emitting barrels of "pork" for local enrichment, will lose its attractiveness.

For starters, we can create, re-create, our own "village." There are several ways of doing this. We sometimes put it to our business students, for one approach, that the best (quick) way to figure out if what they're about to do is ethical, is to imagine that a complete account of what they are doing, along with their reasons for doing it, will appear tomorrow on the front page of *The New York Times* (or, for the graduate students, *The Wall Street Journal*). That simple test puts them back in the (virtual) village – everyone knows what you are doing, and why, so *now* how do you feel about it? The test as it stands is incomplete; all it does is refer the student back to his own conscience, and his perception of the consciences that surround him. That is, indeed, all that is needed for the moral authority of the village. But students raised without villages, and we get more and more of them, may just as likely be happy to think of their depredations exposed for all the world to see – shows what kind of man they are! So the *Wall Street Journal* test, as it is generally known in business circles, will work only when we can presuppose a village, at least in the distant past, which often as not we can no longer do. While it would be a good idea to use that test more, and extend and universalize it and make it real, there will have to be more that we can do to restore our students, fellow citizens, and ourselves, to moral society.

Another approach is that taken by Alcoholics Anonymous, which assembles a caring community around one (and only one) aspect of moral life, to provide real feedback and real support for the moral life. It is limited, but it is effective, to those who join. In many ways, the AA approach recreates the neighborhood church; impelled by a sense of a power whose work in our lives deserves acknowledgment, we gather in certain ritualized ways to recognize that common sense. Once assembled, the church is empowered to minister to the needs of individuals as they come up, and to serve as a catalyst, on occasion, for the formation and empowerment of task forces aimed at improving the life of the community. All of this is good: as such caring communities surround and reinforce the life of the individual, they make it easier for him to stand against the forces in the marketplace that tempt to corruption; as the same communities stimulate activity in the wider society, they create new avenues of stewardship of earth and each other.

A third approach is to attempt to recreate the old local neighborhood, concerted action by concerted action – a small community garden, a block party, a campaign to preserve some open space – until a community of many common interests has been created, which can serve as a forum, a public space, in which to construct informed opinion on the issues of the day. The local action approach approximates the recreation of the Jeffersonian town – a nonsectarian, secular, association of those whose material life together suggests cooperation at several levels. This is the start of the Republic, the civic association, devoid of Church, tradition, prescription or hierarchy, that Alexis de Toqueville concluded was the defining characteristic of America.

All of these approaches, religious or secular, contrast with the standard method of group formation, the assembly of an "interest group" – a collection of people who will work together on a common cause because they already have strong opinions on the matter and seek allies. The trouble with an interest group, for our purposes, is that it cannot change its mind; it represents one point of view only, and the open, self-informing, debate is cut off. An interest group only wants to hear one side of the story. By now we need, we really need, people interested in hearing all sides of the story.

Worse than the interest group, for these purposes, is the "belief" group, the group self-designated by religious or ideological commitment, accepting only true believers and using every instrument of moral coercion to make sure that orthodoxy, of whatever kind, is observed. (The "belief" group, so understood, is in stark contrast to the caring community that a church can be; see above.) The influence of these orthodox associations on the political scene in twenty-first century America is very strong indeed, surprisingly strong; their influence on the corporate scene is negligible. That fact in itself leaves a puzzling loose string, a question mark, in any account of the corporate scandals: given the close connections among the political and the corporate powers during this period of scandal (the connections between the Bush White House and Enron, for instance), and the close connections between the "religious Right" and the same White House, wouldn't we have expected some of Christian morality to affect the corporate scene? Yet there is no evidence of any connection whatsoever.

Learning to Tell the Truth

Our *third* task is to reacquaint ourselves with reality. We are currently in an administration, and an age, which has made a virtue of "denial" – once a technical term of psychology, it has become a ruling ideology of our culture. "Denial" means a determination, probably but not necessarily subconscious, not to believe something that is clearly before your face and in your line of vision, simply because the belief would be too painful for you. In its simplest form, it is the object of pity – the mother who refuses to believe that her child is dead after seeing him in the coffin. In its normal form, it is the object of alarm and frustration – the alcoholic who will not see that she drinks too much, or the aging skier who will not admit that the fastest trails are not safe for him. In its most distressing current form, we still struggle for a reaction – when the officials elected to discern the dangers facing the people, by themselves or in company with as many other experts as it takes, will not *see* and will not *understand* evidence on climate change, the fate of a foreign adventure, the dangers posed by a powerful hurricane, or the ascendancy of the Chinese. A taste for agreeable falsehood rather than unpleasant truth is universal among humanity, but we should learn in early childhood that we cannot indulge that taste, not and continue in the company of intelligent companions. Apparently there are many who attain physical adulthood without learning that lesson. When only their own careers are at stake, the result of denial is regrettable and very hard on the family; when they are the officials in charge of administering war and peace, law and order, guns, butter and taxes, the result of denial is 2,000+ American military dead, billions spent on fruitless adventures, and a deficit that reaches into the trillions. We must have truth or die.

Much of the trouble that the corporations got into in the course of the scandals resulted from the same pattern of denial, in two forms. One is the unadorned insistence on believing the preferred proposition instead of the true proposition – if it works for me, if I like it, it has to be right. If it makes money, there's nothing that can be wrong with it, even if the falsehood of the statements in the annual report is as clear as a beam in the eye. The second is a denial based on the arrogance of the current crop of Masters of the Universe: "since we are the most intelligent, the most forward-thinking, the most important people on earth, it cannot be that we could be caught in our falsehoods and brought to justice. No one would dare stop us." Both denials collapsed in the end, but not until they had cost the investors millions, collapsed enterprises that had provided thousands of jobs, and confronted the country with a spectacle of criminal millionaires stashing their ill-gotten gains while the defrauded employees walked out of the building unemployed and impoverished.

Truth is one standard that can be externally enforced; if the CEO will not tell the truth, if the Board of Directors cannot bring itself to either, then we can find people who will. A firm standard of true representation should be required of corporations (transparency in all doings), ombudsmen and ethics officers should be independent and empowered, and media should be encouraged to play a useful rather than a mischievous part in the public forum. We need to recreate the tradition of strong, independent accounting, auditors of unimpeachable integrity – we had them before, we should be able to have them again. There will continue to be a problem in deciding who will pay for these independent auditors and ombudsmen; the old system, of having the auditing firms paid by the firms that they are auditing, may no longer work. Institutional innovation will be required to supply the new forms of transparency – but this is just the sort of innovation that America is best at. We know that this can be done.

Regaining the Duty of Stewardship

The *fourth* task is a rearticulation of, and recommitment to, a sense of stewardship. The obligation known as "stewardship" is quasi-fiduciary, implying that the "steward" or agent has been entrusted by the "owner," master, or principal, with a single task, or with a cure, in the ancient sense of the word – a body of people, a piece of property, or both, to care for them and to ensure their prosperity and the fulfillment of their purposes. Stewardship starts at the simplest level: I am my master's servant, my master has left the property and all the employees in my care while he is on his travels; in that form the "steward" shows up frequently among the parables in the Gospels. Incidentally, in many of those parables, those charged with stewardship betray the master – faithless tenants of the vineyard (Matthew 22:33–41), less than adequate managers of talents (Matthew 25:14–30), and the dishonest steward of Luke 16, noted above. But the expectations of stewardship were plain in ancient times, and remain so today. At a larger level, the Board of Directors and the executives of any corporation have the same duty of stewardship toward their corporate enterprise, toward the investors who have entrusted their money to the corporation, to the employees who depend on the solvency of the corporation for their daily bread, and to the customers and the community at large who depend on the corporation for quality of the product and revenue from the profits. It's a simple duty to conceive of, but a full time job to carry out. At the largest level, we are all stewards of the earth and the communities we have inherited. The levels of stewardship are all connected; it is a recognized fact that "he who has been faithful in a little, will be faithful in much" (Matthew 25:21). The first task is acknowledgement of the duty, the recognition that we have in fact inherited, not invented, our earth and our families, that to a large extent we have been given, not earned, our companions, our abilities, and the positions of authority we may hold at any given time. We are surely stewards of any enterprises in which, through our own choice, we may participate and whose rewards we claim as our own. We are responsible for the preservation and success of these enterprises; we are accountable to customers, investors, communities and God.

One area where we may ask our leaders to rediscover their duties is the entire realm of business enterprise, which promised us so much at one time, and on which we have, possibly unwisely, depended to provide us with our living. Another major area, forgotten in the rush to material enrichment, is the earth itself, and the fragile ecosystem in which we live and will die, maybe sooner rather than later. The statistics showing the extent to which human activity, intensifying and globalizing, has devastated the earth, are truly horrifying. This is not the place to rehearse them; as with the details of the corporate scandals, others have cleared that path, and some of their work appears in the Appendix to this essay. Suffice it to say, that about half the human damage to the earth's sustaining systems, and about half the human consumption of the world's resources, occurred between the beginning of the human race and the year 1950; the other half has occurred since 1950; and the rate of destruction continues to accelerate. Here, again, we have the pattern of self-reinforcing corruption: those who most stand to benefit from inadequate protection of the environment have purchased political power and friendship, from which position they control the legislation (like the 1872 Mining Law) that protects their profits, portions of which they use to purchase yet more power and protection of their interests. Somewhere the cycle of corruption must be broken, in the realm of environmental protection as well as in the realm of business enterprise; somehow, the duty to protect and preserve the resources that we have been given, human and nonhuman, must be rediscovered.

Re-Visioning the Republic

The *fifth* task is a restatement of the Republic. We need to regain the confidence to articulate a notion of the common good, and the energy to work for it. It might help us to consider the Republic that Thomas Jefferson envisioned.

Jefferson always started with the village, the small (agricultural) town. He presumed a free market in goods and services, and didn't worry very much about keeping the yeoman farmers and tradesmen virtuous – the neighbors would see to that. Each family's affairs were its own. But the town had a certain amount of public business to transact – public safety, fire protection, maintenance of the roads and provision of schools come to mind. To decide these affairs, the town's citizens – read, landowners – would meet, talk the matter over, and make the necessary decisions. They could be counted on, said Jefferson's theory, to be good stewards of the public money, because they had already shown themselves to be good stewards of property on their own account (or else they would not still be landowners). Their sense of responsibility, honed to excellence in the tasks of caring for family, hired help, apprentices, animals, farmland and buildings, easily transferred to the collective responsibility of the town. To govern the state, each town selected someone to represent them, someone whom they had seen in action, whose care for his own property they could observe, whose wisdom they had had an opportunity to test in council, and whom they therefore trusted to represent their interests fairly – or so said the theory. (In practice, corruption had already been invented.) The village was not, for that representative, merely a spiritual or moral presence; the village made sure that he was under constant observation, and if he did not represent their interests well, a few years later he would be replaced with someone who would. On the same principles, the state legislators then chose the members of their body to represent the state at the federal level. Electors chosen from each state elected the President. In theory, at no point in this process did any political choice turn on image, or advertising, or even campaign promises; the choice was made on observed ability only.

The Republic never worked quite that way, for many reasons. Sufficient among the reasons is the ironic failure of visibility and responsible accountability that Jefferson had placed at the heart of governance; distant state capitals rapidly generated the precursors of the smoke-filled rooms that corrupted politics well into the twentieth century. But even in the campaign rhetoric, until recent years, the notion has been preserved, that elected officials shall operate in full sight of those who elected them, and that their major concern shall be the stewardship of the Republic that they have inherited. In this sense, they must be Conservatives – not in the degraded contemporary sense of the word, as signifying hatred of all cultural differences and worshipful deference toward all money, but in the classic sense of protectors of the physical and cultural heritage of our civilization.

What should the protectors protect? They should protect the entirety of the common weal, every aspect of their life together, with reverence for the past, with clear-eyed determination for the present, and with a powerful concern for the future. Note that in this chapter, to this point, no political content has been suggested – it is up to the reader (and the reader's neighbors) to decide what welfare levels should be, and how much should be spent on health care as opposed to education. But two important mandates are intrinsic to the moral burden of the argument:

The first mandate specifies the content of the responsibility or cure, the heritage that must be attended to; it requires at least three efforts at conservation, which can be easily summarized as past, present, and future (material, human, and spiritual). First, we must take care of the earth, the physical substratum of our lives together, to protect it from all the horrors of overexploitation that render it ugly, unproductive, and eventually poisonous

– deforestation, erosion, extinction of native species, pollution, desertification. Additionally, we must take care of the built environment, the deposit of history, the heritage of beauty and permanence that has been left us by previous generations. Those who conserve must be conservationists, in the broadest sense of the term. Second, we must take care of each other; where there is enough food to go around, there is no excuse for allowing some members of the community to starve, or to live in a manner which is demeaning or degrading to their humanity. Everyone should be fed, housed, and (for the sake of the rich as well as the poor) given adequate medical care, as long as the resources are available in the community. This mandate should not come as a surprise: it is the custom of most villages, and dictated by Christianity, still the majority religion in the United States. The enjoyment of affluence, as it has been said, in a context of poverty, is a situation of sin; in the clear message of the Gospels, no Christian can rest content with a situation where some enjoy great wealth and others suffer from poverty. (Self-interest alone propels the Christian to care for the unfortunate. For Christ's understanding of what will happen to people who ignore the hungry, the homeless, those sick and in prison, see the Gospel according to St. Matthew, 25:31–46. It's not pleasant.) Third, we must protect the future of the community, by ensuring that the children born will be raised with a sense of their responsibilities to the community, and with an education that prepares them for a world more technologically sophisticated than we would be able to conceive. That education must incorporate more than the technological skills they will need; we must make sure that it incorporates the narratives of their several communities, so that they will be able to care for their heritage in their generation, and transmit it intact to generations yet unborn.

The second mandate is procedural. Whatever we decide, we must decide consciously and together. Aristotle was convinced that the very process of coming to public decisions – negotiating, adjudicating, balancing many points of view in order to come to the decision that would benefit the *polis* as a whole – was the most characteristically human activity and the highest function in our nature (always excepting the life of pure contemplation, which by its very nature had to be the privilege of the very few). When he said that "Man [better translation: a Human] is a political animal," what he meant was that a human reached fulfillment, became entirely human, in the context of a Greek *polis*, with Athens specifically in mind. What it was to live in the *polis* is made clearer in Pericles's funeral address in Thucydides's *Peloponnesian Wars*: the citizen was expected to take full part in all the activities of the city. "We do not say, of him who takes no part in public life, that he 'minds his own business.' We say he has no business here at all." Aristotle, in the third book of the *Politics*, spells that out: a citizen must not only attend the assembly, and presumably vote on the issues that came up, he must also serve on juries, act as a judge on occasion, and hold other political offices as appropriate. The point was that the citizen must "rule and be ruled in turn": when not holding office, must understand the difficulties and problems of government, and so cooperate loyally more than a mere king's subject would; and when holding office, must understand the problems of the ordinary citizen that he was but a few days ago – and avoid all arrogance, all presumption, all of the greed and usurpations and unjustified perquisites with which we have seen our own elected and appointed officers indulge themselves. Again, the key to accountability is visibility; the city is small, terms of office are short, and memories are long. Aristotle and Pericles understood that an active, informed, vigilant citizenry, experienced in the holding of political offices at the local level, is the best guarantee of honest government. It was then, and it still is.

Ending the Crime Wave

Our *sixth* task, to return to the corporate scandals, is to end the crime, especially the inexcusable crime of those in the most privileged positions in the nation. To the best of our ability, we must re-create a society where we are not ashamed to affirm and reinforce moral ideals, and to hold even the paragons of business accountable to them. With villages in place, at least in our own lives, with a functioning republic, we should have rather less trouble than we seem to have had recently in discovering the political will to stop the white-collar criminals in their tracks, and set them on the road to honest dealing. There is a law, and no one, no matter how rich, is above it.

At this point, for the first time, citizens may be in a position to address the problem of greed directly. The elephant in the living room, that we have tiptoed around in all of our efforts to describe the scandals, is not the illegality of the accounting, or of the loans, or of the offshore SPEs. The elephant is the simple greed that led these highly placed officials to commit certain illegal acts, but much more prominently, to accept millions, tens of millions of dollars, each year, while lobbying to be released from obligations to provide pensions for their workers and provide outplacement for the workers who had been laid off in order to raise the price of the stock in order to secure bonuses, over and above the high salaries, for the same overpaid executives. We forget, sometimes, that we have a reasonable sense of what is appropriate in the way of material compensation. There is a reason why Kozlowski's $6,000 shower curtain keeps coming up in the literature of the scandals. Allowing for inflationary slippage over time – remember when Cadillacs were the most expensive car on the market at $2,000? – we still tend to know what things are worth and what constitutes paying too much for the sake of vulgar display. There are rules in other countries that we could adopt here: the salaries of the top executives can easily be pegged to the average yearly income of the lowest-paid worker, or a multiple of the average hourly worker's wage. But the "compensation committees" of the Boards of Directors of our major corporations tend to be composed of Directors who themselves are salaried (and bonused and stock optioned) in other similar companies, and have good reason to expect generous treatment in exchange for generous treatment – and in exchange for a responsible stinginess, who knows what kind of retaliation might be feared? We have empowered the cronies to reward the cronies, and they are doing just that.

Could we, as the citizens of the United States, ever confront the issue directly? There would be the catcalls, and the protests that we were practicing a "politics of envy," initiating "class warfare," as if that were not the name for the systematic transfer of wealth from the poor to the rich that we have watched since the 1980s. But if we can find the political and moral will, we can decide to cap the top salaries and "bonuses," not to mention stock options, of the very rich. We may expect two rewards, for starters. First, we will save the shareholders untold millions of dollars – if they can't use the millions to reward the executives, maybe the Board will return the savings to the investors? That would be nice. Second, without the motivation of bonuses for stock performance, possibly the executives will stop misstating earnings in order to send the stock higher – for, sadly, it turns out that those generous stock options correlate positively with the tendency of the executives to overstate the earnings of the company.

Those two immediate benefits will be followed by others. Third, we may expect higher executive satisfaction with the results of their annual competition for the highest compensation in the country. We must remember that CEOs (and other executives), like basketball players, compete for the highest compensation just for the prestige it will bring. Right now, they are in a competition that may be likened to a soccer game without boundaries where each team may play with as many balls as it can purchase – no one can guess ahead of time what any given team's score will be, so anxious competitors have to drive their own score unreasonably high to make sure they are not disgraced in the ultimate announcement of results. But with firm caps in place, their competition with neighboring executives for a prestigious society will occur on a level playing field – they continue to compete, but with clearly understood caps past which they cannot go – and that cannot help but dampen the unlimited, obscene, greed.

At some point, as citizens, we may want to confront the larger problem of anonymous greed and sin in general – the online gambling, online pornography, the vast network of lucrative encouragement of sinful fantasies, which wrecks fortunes and families, but not third parties. That's for a future treatise; the corporate scandals of our time left a trail of cheated victims who were no relation at all to the well-placed criminals, and they deserve justice.

Finding Peace

The *seventh* task, and the last for this treatise, is to articulate a contemporary version of the good life, the life that we actually want to live that does not rest on injustice to others. Its roots are ancient. On the temple that covered the cave of the Delphic Oracle, according to legend, were two mottos: "Know thyself," essentially meaning "know your own limits, and be humble," which was Socrates's favorite, and "Nothing in excess," around which Aristotle developed his moral philosophy.

The way to the realization of this life, the path to peace, circles through all our lines of argument so far, and serves as a good review. We begin with the insight, spelled out above, that we are communal before we are individual – thought and reasoning are born of conversations, self-consciousness is born of group interaction, and above all, individual morality is the internalized morality of the successive communities, "villages," of our experience. Villages are very strong: we have ample proof that the hardwired tendencies of greed and violence can be kept under control quite adequately by any established community, and that experimental communities (Mennonites, for instance) have been able to raise peacefulness and simplicity to heroic levels, maintained for generations. Where violence and greed are confronted early, shown to be unnecessary for survival and sure to draw community disapproval on every occasion, simplicity of life is not that difficult to maintain.

But are we sure that this way of life is a universal ideal? How many of us could, even if we would, live in such "ideal" communities? Think of the sacrifice involved: the only way such communities can survive is through deliberate isolation, through very careful monitoring of all experiences of all the community, to ensure that only experiences conducive to their ideal are possible. (We are reminded of Plato's *Republic* again, this time of the education of the Guardians – whose every line of poetry and bar of music had to be screened for the appropriate martial quality!)

This is surely one way of attaining an ideally simple life, but we may note that very few communities have elected to follow this route. If we value, at all, the restless quality of human curiosity, that continually reaches out to explore the outer boundaries of its experience, we might hope that we can live a moderate life without such physical, cultural and intellectual isolation.

There is another possibility. Here one of the most interesting features of the communal characteristic of humans takes center stage: the human imagination can be employed to supply witnessing communities where actual, physically located, groups are lacking – St. Paul's "cloud of witnesses," the community of those living and dead who somehow provide support to the individual in the absence of real and present people. We all know the way such witnesses, such communities, work. This last year I had a student from a very poor family who had worked his way through school on the night shift of the supermarket, graduating Phi Beta Kappa, Magna Cum Laude. We asked him what had kept him going, and he said, "My mother. I worked so hard because I wanted my mother to be proud of me." She had died when he was 13. The cloud of witnesses is, or can be, as strong as the real village.

Those witnesses account, in large part, for the fact that individual integrity, strong enough to stand against the crowd and turn back all temptation, while very rare, *does* exist. Where does it come from? Apparently, from the nurturing of the communities, actual and imagined, natural and constructed, with which we surround ourselves. The reciprocity that Aristotle insisted on for his real city, where the responsibility for nurturing goodness is evenly held by city and citizen, who are responsible for each other, shows up again on the level of communities of the spirit. It is my job to examine even the communities that strengthen me, real and ideal, to make sure that they stay honest and will guide me in the right paths. (Realistically, all I can ask of them is that they make me fear the wrong path for fear of their disapproval: the *Wall Street Journal* test of rightness.) There is a certain illogic in this description: my community, of whatever sort, is responsible for keeping me honest, and I am responsible for keeping the community honest, and vigilant, and free from taint of corruption or cronyism. But that is how the mutual support of community and individual works; if the system is to foster honesty, that is how it will do it.

From the above, it is our responsibility *first* to join with our neighbors and create actual communities, to nurture our children and ourselves in lives that make sense and are not dominated by fear and greed, *second* to instill in our children, and ourselves, that ideal community of witnesses who will stand as lifelong support for the courses of action we know are right, and *third*, following from (not preceding) those, to maintain a reasoned public dialogue on the course that the society should take in conformity with the moral consensus we have developed. The unlimited indulgence of uncontrolled greed helps no one, even the one indulged, just as the unlimited indulgence of uncontrolled violence (as in a terrorist society) destroys everything it might have wanted to build. Its control will be one of the first items on the agenda of any functioning society.

The quarrels over which regulation will do the most good or anyway the least harm, and if there should be caps on executive (or other) compensation, where should they be, and should we change the tax laws and if so how, form no essential part of the reform of an America wallowing in the shame of her own corruption. The steps to be taken to remedy the present scandals and prevent the next ones wind back along the path I have traced. We must restore the moral community, restore its mission of producing and sustaining the virtuous individual, and engage those individuals in their turn in the truly political activity of stewardship, of the earth, the community, and of their fellow human beings. When we have done that, we will have restored peace and self-restraint at both the community and the individual level, and in that simplicity we will be able to live in peace.

Even now there is a growing literature of self-restraint. The "voluntary simplicity" movement, which began with St. Francis of Assisi and continues today, not just among the Mennonites, has spawned a very large literature, starting in contemporary terms in the 1960s; some of it appears in the bibliography. There are even books aimed directly at the business executive, notably among them Laura Nash and Howard Stevenson's *Just Enough*, the thesis of which is that you will live a much happier and more fulfilling life if you aim at a success that is proportionate to your loves and limits, which balances your commitments in a way that fits.[1]

The trouble with most of this literature is that it is too Platonic, following the argument of Plato's *Republic* (source of the story of Gyges and the ring, in chapter 1 above). In the *Republic*, Plato presents an excellent and persuasive argument that even without social sanctions, reason alone will tell us that we ought to live a moral life even if we could get away with an immoral one. We'll just be happier. The proof is valid. In the simplicity literature, work after work proves the same: limit your desires and be happy and be free. Nash and Stevenson prove the same. But that

---

[1]   Laura Nash and Howard Stevenson, both of the Harvard Business School, *Just Enough: Tools for Creating Success in Your Work and Life* (New York: John Wiley and Sons, 2004).

never was the problem, was it? Even if an extended proof of the greater happiness of the life of self-restraint is difficult, we have so much evidence closer to home. There is no difficulty convincing a young drug addict that he will be happier if he renounces drugs; most alcoholics will agree that their lives would be much better and happier if they stopped drinking. But it is not the rational argument that stops the alcoholic from drinking; it is the community of Alcoholics Anonymous or similar structure that provides him with the motivation, the support, and above all the accountability to the group on a regular – daily or weekly – basis, that makes the life of restraint possible.[2]

Reason will not lead us to peace. For that we need a community. To restrain our natural greed, it helps to know that great amounts of money will not make us happy, at least if we pursue money to the exclusion of other goods in our lives. Yes, that can be proved, by Plato and Laura Nash and many, many others in between. It really helps, even more, to see that all the others to whom we compare ourselves, and whose admiration we desire, similarly exercise self-restraint and do not steal even when presented with an opportunity to steal. But at the beginning and at the end, what helps my self-restraint most is the eyes of the witnesses, all the people around me, which render clandestine theft physically

---

[2] AA is an excellent example of the kind of community-building, if only, here, for a special purpose – going from the mere existence of a group, to group procedures, highly formalized, found in practice to be effective in achieving the group's objectives, to a literature that provides support when the recovering alcoholic is far from the meeting. The price, that is paid to maintain the effectiveness of the group in controlling an otherwise intractable addiction, is that AA cannot use its group strength to accomplish other worthy goals, for instance in politics.

impossible for so long that eventually the temptation does not bother to surface any more. This is why two ushers are required to count the church offering on Sunday morning. There could not be more honest and virtuous people in the world, yet two of them are required to count the offering every Sunday morning.

A Concluding Note

We always hope to "learn the lessons" of a period of scandal. I suggest above that if by "learning our lessons" we mean that we won't be greedy anymore, we've learned nothing. On the other hand, maybe we can learn again to confront the horrific results of unbridled greed calmly, rationally, but with an unswerving passion for justice. We have done this, as a people, several times in our history, most recently in the 1930s, when the great regulatory structures (that we have just dismantled) were put in place. For the most part, these amounted to rules requiring two ushers to count the money and report to the SEC if there seemed to be systematic discrepancies. The regulations were, in the language of the corporation, "burdensome." Further, they were not perfect; thieves could squeak through the cracks, and some results were irrational. Yes, but they worked: first, they announced to the world and to the children, the generations not yet in the community of trade and citizenry, that we intended to run business honestly, and taught them to form their education and their expectations on that basis. Second, they announced to those starting and continuing careers in business that there was a cloud of witnesses urging them on to honesty, a country that cared about the honor of the profession of business, for the sake of which honor they would not cheat. And third, to the recalcitrant lords of business who had caused the trouble in the first place, they announced that earthly representatives of that cloud of witnesses would be available to the prosecutor for testimony should the prosecutor require it. On the whole, it was a very healthy balance. We have done it before, and with the political will that we have a duty to muster and every right to exercise, we shall do it again.

Thank you very much.

Bibliography

Barreveld, Dirk J. *The Enron Collapse: Creative Accounting, Wrong Economics or Criminal Acts?* San Jose: Writers Club Press, 2002.

Bogle, John C. *The Battle For the Soul of Capitalism.* New Haven: Yale University Press, 2005.

Briody, Dan. *The Halliburton Agenda: The Politics of Oil and Money.* Hoboken, NJ: John Wiley and Sons, 2004.

Cassidy, John. "The World of Business: The Greed Cycle, or How the Financial System Encouraged Corporations to Go Crazy." *The New Yorker*, September 23, 2002, pp. 64–77.

Cassidy, John. "Annals of Finance: The Investigation. How Eliot Spitzer Humbled Wall Street." *The New Yorker*, April 7, 2003, pp. 55–73.

Cruver, Brian. *Anatomy of Greed: The Unshredded Truth from an Enron Insider.* New York: Carroll and Graf, 2002.

Duffy, Michael. "What Did They Know and When Did They Know It? Meet Sherron Watkins, Who Sounded the Alarm on Enron Long Before its Collapse." *Time*, January 28, 2002, pp. 16–22.

Eichenwald, Kurt. *Conspiracy of Fools: A True Story.* New York: Broadway Books, 2005. By all accounts, this one is the best.

Elliott, A. Larry and Richard J. Schroth. *How Companies Lie: Why Enron Is Just the Tip of the Iceberg (The Investor's Guide to Corporate Smoke and Mirrors).* New York: Crown Business Briefings, 2002.

BIBLIOGRAPHY

Fox, Loren. *Enron: The Rise and Fall.* Hoboken, NJ: John Wiley and Sons, 2003.

Fusaro, Peter C. and Ross M. Miller. *What Went Wrong at Enron: Everyone's Guide to the Largest Bankruptcy in U.S. History.* Hoboken: John Wiley & Sons, 2002.

Korten, David. "The Difference Between Money and Wealth: How Out-of-Control Speculation is Destroying Real Wealth." *The American Prospect,* January–February 1999, p. 4.

Lizza, Ryan. "White House Watch: World Away." *The New Republic,* July 22, 2002, pp. 24–5. George W. Bush's dealings with Harken are eerily prescient of the entire Enron scandal.

Lowenstein, Roger. "We Regret to Inform You That You No Longer Have a Pension: America's Next Financial Debacle." ("The End of Pensions?") *The New York Times Magazine,* October 30, 2005, pp. 56ff.

Machan, Tibor R. and James E. Chesher. *A Primer on Business Ethics.* New York: Rowman and Littlefield, 2002.

McLean, Bethany and Peter Elkind. *The Smartest Guys in the Room: The Amazing Rise and Scandalous Fall of Enron.* New York: Penguin Portfolio, 2003.

Toffler, Barbara Ley with Jennifer Reingold. *Final Accounting: Ambition, Greed, and the Fall of Arthur Andersen.* New York: Broadway Books, 2003.

Index